Victorian Critical Interventions
Donald E. Hall, Series Editor

Novel Professions

Interested Disinterest and the Making of the Professional in the Victorian Novel

JENNIFER RUTH

The Ohio State University Press
Columbus, Ohio

Library of Congress Cataloging-in-Publication Data
Ruth, Jennifer.
Novel professions : interested disinterest and the making of the professional in the Victorian novel / Jennifer Ruth.
p. cm.—(Victorian critical interventions)
Includes bibliographical references and index.
ISBN 0–8142–1016–3 (alk. paper)—ISBN 0–8142–5152–8 (pbk. : alk. paper)—ISBN 0–8142–9092–2 (cd-rom) 1. English fiction—19th century—History and criticism. 2. Professions in literature. 3. Dickens, Charles, 1812–1870. David Copperfield. 4. Trollope, Anthony, 1815–1882. Three clerks. 5. Brontë, Charlotte, 1816–1855. Professor. 6. Criticism—History—21st century. I. Title. II. Series.
PR878.P726R88 2006
823.'809352—dc22
2005024810

Type set in Adobe Garamond.
Cover design by Dan O'Dair.
Printed by Thomson-Shore, Inc.

The paper used in this publication meets the minimum requirements of the American National Standard for Information Sciences—Permanence of Paper for Printed Library Materials. ANSI Z39.48–1992.
9 8 7 6 5 4 3 2 1

Contents

Acknowledgments

Studying the professional did not make me one: Nancy Armstrong deserves the credit for that. I feel enormously lucky to have worked with her and to still have the benefit of her wisdom whenever the need arises. Ellen Rooney and Tamar Katz read this book in its very earliest stage, and I thank them for their thorough, thoughtful readings. Sarah Winter and Elaine Hadley graciously included me in the "Locating the Victorians" Conference in London in 2001, at which I delivered a part of chapter 3, and I've been grateful for their support ever since. Cathy Shuman and Anita Levy inspired some of this work and kindly read some of it as well. Nicholas Daly, Caroline Reitz, and Danny Hack make me glad I joined this profession. Thanks also to Bruce Robbins and Jim English for generously commenting on chapters when I approached them out of the blue.

I am grateful to David Goslee for inviting me to speak in the "New Voices" Lecture Series at the University of Tennessee at Knoxville in 2003. The UT English department proved an engaged and engaging audience for the book's introduction, and the book benefited from their response. In particular, thanks to Allen Dunn for his brain-teaser of a question and for our dialogue about Bourdieu.

At Portland State, Peter Carafiol has served as my advisor-in-residence, helping me in ways too numerous to recount. I'd also like to give particular thanks to Elisabeth Ceppi, Lorraine Mercer, Maria Depriest, Tracy Dillon, Leerom Medovoi, Marcia Klotz, Amy Greenstadt, Maude Hines, Sue Danielson, Ann Marie Fallon, Katya Amato, John Smyth, and Greg Goekjian. Of the many PSU students to whom I'm grateful, I'd like to single out Chris Hall, Alex Davis, Steve Sherman, and Brian Jennings for giving me their time as researchers or readers.

I want to thank Donald Hall for the grace with which he serves as editor of the Victorian Critical Interventions Series and the first-rate staff of The Ohio State University Press: Heather Lee Miller, Sandy Crooms, and Maggie Diehl. Chapter 1 originally appeared as "Between Labor and Capital: Charlotte Brontë's Professional Professor" in *Victorian Studies* (Winter 2003). It won the INCS 2003 Essay Prize. The second section of chapter 2 appeared as "Mental Capital, Industrial Time, and the Professional in *David Copperfield*" in *Novel: A Forum on Fiction* (Summer 1999).

Countless things personal and professional were likely pressing for John Plotz's attention—for one, his second baby was due in days—and yet he wrote the most brilliant and encouraging reader's report imaginable. I have not managed to do all that you envisioned for *Novel Professions,* John, but that vision has made the book much better even so. Thanks also are owed that other fantastic Victorianist, my fellow Brown alumnus and dear friend Ivan Kreilkamp. Finally, thank you to those people who make life worthwhile: Sara Levine and Chris Gaggero, my parents John and Charlotte Ruth, and my favorite little person, Charlotte Cowan-Ruth. This book is for my favorite big person, Scott Cowan.

Introduction

> The problem with this final avatar of bourgeois privilege, the meritocratic system—the problem, that is, from the point of view of the bourgeoisie—is that it is the least (not the most) defensible, because its basis is the thinnest. The oppressed may swallow being ruled by and giving reward to those who are to the manner born. But being ruled by and giving reward to people whose only asserted claim (and that a dubious one) is that they are smarter, that is too much to swallow.
>
> —Immanuel Wallerstein

"Smart Kids" is the special topic of a recent issue of *the minnesota review.* Guest-editor Renny Christopher begins by confessing, "I was a smart kid. I was officially identified as a smart kid by the IQ test I took in the fourth grade" (111). Ashamed at having fallen for this magical conferral of identity, she writes, "Now I wish I could go back and kick my nine-year old self in the butt and say, 'don't fall for that crap!'" She discusses a friend who, when the subject of the special issue arose, explained how she had been a "dumb kid" and had proudly acted out all the behaviors associated with that label just as Christopher had performed the good-girl attributes associated with hers. This friend "told a story," continues Christopher, "about how she, as a working-class kid, won the respect of other working-class kids in her school—by rebelling and sassing the teachers. Once, a teacher literally picked her up by the arms, carried her out into the hall, and slammed her against the lockers. . . . I was thinking, wow, that's so cool and envying Barbara for having had the balls to defy authority like that, to be a bad kid, rather than the disgusting little conformist that I was, respecting teachers' authority . . . playing by the rules, wanting approval from those authorities, being the perfect little fascist subject, not the brave defiant little revolutionary that Barbara was"

(111–12). If the IQ test "officially" decreed her smartness, then "I now officially and publicly renounce [it]," Christopher writes, "and declare my readiness to do penance for having so enthusiastically and unthinkingly (and dumbly?) accepted the smart kid mantle" (112). In Christopher's piece, the dumb kids turn out to be smart and the smart kids turn out to be dupes.[1] Having "swallowed hook, line, sinker, and fishing pole" the notion of her own innate ability, Christopher surfaces only to find she's drowning in bourgeois conformity (111). Her unique individuality, her "special" IQ, was simply the professional-managerial class molding her in its own image (111).

The easy response to Christopher's self-flagellation is "poor little smart kid" but her distress is genuine—"kick my . . . self," "disgusting little conformist," "perfect little fascist," "do penance"—and her honesty admirable. She only says in personal terms what numerous literary critics say in more disguised form. Rather, I begin with "Smart Kids" to pose the question: Why do we literary critics say, with so much passion and so much resentment against our recent past, against our present, and against ourselves, that we are no better—that we are, in fact, worse—than everyone else?

Christopher takes it for granted that her academic success (now redefined as conformist failure) in contrast to her less-educated brother can be traced to that fateful fourth-grade IQ test, but one could imagine the trajectories of brother and sister playing out quite differently (and, indeed, within the implicit terms of her essay, how to account for her friend whose defiant dumb-kid past did not stop her from growing up to be Christopher's colleague?). Recent research in the psychology of motivation suggests that affirmations of innate intelligence often have counterintuitive effects, with those told they possess superior ability less likely to pursue challenging tasks and more likely to abandon tasks once they prove difficult.[2] After all, if you try and fail, you might lose the "smart" mantle altogether, whereas if you never try, you just did not "apply" yourself. What drops out of Christopher's account—and becomes dangerous for the individual anxious about his or her smart identity—is effort, labor, work. Presumably, Christopher worked fairly hard to get her PhD, but this effort is summarily discounted. By ignoring all that came between the IQ test and her current post as a professor, does she not run the risk of reproducing the illusion she is at pains to dispel, the illusion upon which the IQ test rests? That ability can be abstracted from effort?

By its end, the Victorian period gave us not only Sigmund Freud but the Simon-Binet test, the prototype of the IQ test first introduced in 1905.[3] The idea that there was something called inherent intelligence that might be objectively measured allowed the educational system to sort students into vocational or professional tracks. Where Freud made us a mystery to ourselves, the IQ test stamped us with objective value—a seemingly straightforward, allegedly irrefutable measure of our cognitive worth. Am I smart or must I rely on effort? But how did the two—ability and effort—become separable categories in the first place? Apparently, the line between them had been drawn at least by 1875, when James Cotter Morison devoted an essay in the *Fortnightly Review* to complaining about it. He said with exasperation, "There is something offensive and even harmful in the antithesis set up between genius and learning, as if the one almost necessarily excluded the other, and as if the man of learning were, by nature of the case, a hard-working dunce who strove, by accumulating knowledge, not only to make up for his deficiency in talent, but to acquire an unfounded claim to some of its honours" (537). Terms like "effort" and "intelligence" get separated and reified and then muddled again in the middle decades of the nineteenth century, the exchange between cousins Sir Francis Galton and Charles Darwin being a condensed case in point. After reading Galton's book *Hereditary Genius* (1869), Darwin wrote him: "You have made a convert of an opponent in one sense, for I have always maintained that, excepting fools, men did not differ much in intellect, only in zeal and hard work." Galton replied: "Character, including the aptitude for hard work, is inheritable like every other faculty" (*Memories* 290). Congratulated for abstracting a capacity from effort, Galton extended his nominalizing grasp to "effort," which then itself becomes a kind of capacity—"being" disentangled from "doing," "doing" morphs into another kind of "being."[4]

Novel Professions: Interested Disinterest and the Making of the Professional in the Victorian Novel studies the way the Victorians conceived professional identity by drawing and then worrying distinctions between ability and effort, intelligence and merit, and being and doing. "The professions as we know them are very much a Victorian creation," wrote W. J. Reader (2). At the heart of this creation, I argue, lay a tension between being and doing: a tension between the fact that people discover themselves to *be* suited for a certain line of work (via competitive examination, for example) and the fact that they must also over the course of time *do* that work, and thus come to fulfill the promise of their initial discovery. This tension developed over the course of the nineteenth century, but was at its most taut at mid-century, when Victorians begin to conceptualize an emergent professional class. The late 1840s and the 1850s, the period from which I draw my archive, established the cultural conditions for the class's explosion in both numbers and power in the 1860s, 1870s, and 1880s. At the start of the nineteenth century, such careers as law, medicine, and the church drew on both the gentry and upper middle classes but did not produce men who clearly identified themselves as a distinct class.

By the end of the 1850s, however, professionals were an identifiable community gaining in political and social importance, such that ambitious young men required a handbook to aid them in the momentous task of choosing a profession—H. Byerley Thomson's 1857 *The Choice of a Profession: A Concise Account and Comparative Review of the English Professions.* "The importance of the professions can hardly be overrated," Thomson wrote; "They form the head of the great English middle class, maintain its tone of independence, keep up to the mark its standard of morality, and direct its intelligence" (5). A glance at the numbers confirms the mid-century's significance: "Between 1841 and 1881," writes historian Harold Perkin, "professional occupations trebled in number, compared with a two-thirds increase in general population, and came to constitute a substantial element in the middle class" (*Origins* 428–29). By the 1860s, Nancy Armstrong and Leonard Tennenhouse report, "What had seemed a subordinate sector of the middle class made up of managers, professionals, experts of various kinds was running England" (120). Galton's choice of the professions as the ruling principle by which *Hereditary Genius* organizes its statistics on eminent men—beginning, appropriately enough, with judges—is telling evidence for Armstrong and Tennenhouse's claim.

As various disciplines, including fiction-writing, began to professionalize—by defining objective standards of knowledge, developing processes of evaluation and accreditation, and organizing into communities in the form of chapters, associations, and societies—the novel attempted to "theorize" the professional, trying to do what nonfiction failed to do. Political economy could not make sense of this new figure whose stock-in-trade consisted of intangible services. Adam Smith, as well as those after him like David Ricardo and Karl Marx, identified three groups that constituted separate classes: owners of land, owners of capital, and owners of labor. How, then, to account for professionals who perform labor but also possess a kind of capital (mental capital in the form of measurable talent and the stored labor of knowledge acquisition)? The nascent professional also confounded assumptions about the relationship between economic and *social* class: if he did not look or act like a wage laborer, he nevertheless relied upon a wage or a salary; if he did not possess financial capital (though he had to have *some* to embark on a professional career), he claimed what we would now call cultural capital.[5] In short, much of what has made this class notoriously difficult to theorize both then and now is what Erik Olin Wright calls its "contradictory class locations" (quoted in Clarke 67).

If the professional suffers from contradictory class *locations*—neither in the capitalist nor the laborer's camp and yet both a (mental) capitalist and an (intellectual) laborer—then he is also subject to ambiguous, even perhaps ambivalent, *temporalities*—neither born a professional, as the gentry is born gentry, nor self-made, like the Smilesian businessman, and yet both born (with certain aptitudes) and made (through mental effort). With a simultaneously pregnant and collapsed relationship to time, the professional putatively boasts mental "gifts" that anticipate his future (pregnant) but he simply becomes what he was always meant to be (collapsed). Phrenology and then, later, the competitive examination were central to the development of this professionalizing logic. Because they took a static measure of a person that allegedly could predict future success or failure, they provided a way to identify the future professional, the figure with professional promise. Precursors of the IQ test, phrenology and the exam also appeared to act as objective gatekeepers to the professions, counterpoints to patronage and jobbery. By converting "doing" into "being"—not what you learned but what you are capable of learning—they served useful credentialing functions for the modern professional and assured him a place higher in the social hierarchy than the businessman or manual laborer. "Agents are increasingly defined in terms only of *what they do*, by the technically defined skills or tasks that fall under their title or job, the further one descends in the hierarchy," Pierre Bourdieu has written, "and conversely, by *what they are* as one moves up" (*State Nobility* 119). But in this act of social magic, phrenology and the competitive examination seemed to bypass the actual work necessary to earn an identity and, thus, raised thorny epistemological questions for conceptualizing the professional. In all three novels I analyze, this tension between doing and being structures the text's production of a credible (and credentialed) professional, as I show with regard to phrenology in chapter 1 and competitive examination in chapters 2 and 3.

The Victorian novel put phrenology and the competitive examination at the center of the Victorian fantasy of professional identity. Many scholars have explored the way phrenology saturates Victorian novels, but almost none have studied the role of the examination in Victorian fiction. Yet it is hard to imagine certain Dickens novels and virtually any of Anthony Trollope's without the Oxbridge or civil service examinations.[6] Even George Eliot, who generally relied less on shorthand in her elaboration of characters, made sure to introduce Fred Vincy as "the plucked Fred" and to have Fred begin his reformation by finally passing his examinations (158). "The poor young men," commiserates Miss Ilex of *Gryll Grange* (1861) in a conversation about competitive examinations, "are not held qualified for a profession unless they have overloaded their understanding with things of no use in it" (185). "Well, Jackson!" says one fellow in a *Punch* cartoon from 1852 (see figure 1), "You see they've

Rapid Undergraduate. "WELL, JACKSON! YOU SEE THEY 'VE PLUCKED ME AGAIN.

Porter of St. Boniface. "YE-ES, SIR, I WAS VERY SORRY WHEN I 'EARD OF IT, SIR."

Undergraduate. "AH! I DID INTEND GOING INTO THE CHURCH, AND BEING AN ORNAMENT TO THE PROFESSION—BUT AS THEY WON'T LET ME THROUGH—I THINK—I SHALL CUT THE WHOLE CONCERN."

Figure 1

plucked me again." "I did intend going into the Church, and being an Ornament to the Profession—but as they won't let me through—I think—I shall cut the whole concern," he ends, absurdly trying to save face. "My dear Henry," begins one faux letter-writing sister of a more fortunate fellow in another issue of *Punch*, "Mamma and Pappa desire me to say that they were very much gratified at reading that you acquitted yourself so well at the examination, and Pappa has given me a cheque to enclose" (25). Indeed, if we are to trust Pip's account, the competitive examination was the preferred "mental exercise" of even the ragged schools, where the "pupils entered among themselves upon a competitive examination on the subject of Boots, with the view of ascertaining who could tread hardest upon whose toes" (84).

In a culture as mesmerized by sorting and categorization as the Victorians', nobody should be surprised to find the examination playing this central role and yet it has received attention within literary criticism only very recently. In *Pedagogical Economies* (2000), Cathy Shuman analyzes different Victorian authors' use of the exam as a structure to negotiate and legitimize their own labor as readers and writers. In doing so, she articulates economies particular to intellectual labor—pedagogical economies of evaluation and assessment reliant for many of their terms and maneuvers upon those economies that govern the state, the market, or the home but nonetheless distinguishable from them. Although I discovered Shuman's work after completing my own research on competitive examinations, *PE* has greatly enriched *Novel Professions*, deepening my own understanding of the paradoxes of professional identity.

In my study of Victorian fiction's formation of professional identity, I am also indebted to a number of other works that have addressed the nineteenth-century professional and/or the category of intellectual labor. Important touchstones are Bruce Robbins's *Secular Vocations* (1993), Thomas Pfau's *Wordsworth's Profession* (1997), Jonathan Freedman's *Professions of Taste* (1990), Nancy Armstrong and Leonard Tennenhouse's chapter "The Vanishing Intellectual" in *The Imaginary Puritan* (1992), Lawrence Rothfield's *Vital Signs* (1992), and Clifford Siskin's *The Work of Writing* (1998). Alan Mintz's thorough discussion of *Middlemarch*'s portrayal of the rise of the professions in *George Eliot and the Novel of Vocation* saved me from writing a chapter on Eliot while also motivating me to look at novels written when professional identity occupied an earlier stage of manufacture. Published in 1978, Mintz's book offers an interesting glimpse of what studies of the professional looked like before criticism grew suspicious of this world-historical figure. James Eli Adams's analysis in *Dandies and Desert Saints: Styles of Victorian Masculinity* (1995) of the precarious gendering of masculine intellectual labor, and the consequent need for an ascetic rhetoric of self-discipline, also informed my work here, particularly the chapter on *David Copperfield*.

More recently, Daniel Hack's fascinating work on the Royal Literary Fund and "begging writers" and Clare Pettitt's *Patent Inventions* (2004) has assured me that I am pursuing an important thesis. Opening up and carefully developing lines of inquiry that my book does not consider, Hack demonstrates that the Victorian writer's "rejection of the marketplace as the sole or ultimate index of value neither constitutes nor implies a fully professionalistic disavowal of market competition and payment, let alone a modernist embrace of market failure as a source of artistic legitimacy" ("Literary Paupers" 694). *Patent Inventions* appeared as I was preparing *Novel Professions* for press, but in many respects it, too, might be seen to complement and historicize the readings I offer. *Patent Inventions*, Pettitt writes, "takes the current critical discussion of copyright law and the construction of the artist in the Victorian period out of its literary-critical isolation and restores it to the wider debate in the period about labour and value" (2). Literary criticism has typically viewed the Victorian artist within the Kantian and Romantic tradition opposing art to mechanical invention, but Pettitt unearths a widespread discourse in which the artist and the manufacturer functioned as analogues for one another. "By the end of the 1830s," she writes, "analogies between mechanical inventors and literary inventors were commonplace" (5). It is impossible to overstate the value of these contributions as correctives to our current critical tendencies. Once we see that the Victorian artist, and I would add professional, encouraged a metaphoric link between himself and the mechanical inventor, our mode of "exposing" the artist-professional's autonomy as self-serving illusion—a critical routine discussed in greater detail below—loses a great deal of its impetus. In Pettitt and Hack's rigorously historicized scenarios, the Victorian artist-professional underscored his position as market agent as often as he obscured it.[7]

While I see *Novel Professions* following the lead of Shuman, Hack, and Pettitt, I also view it as part of the growing body of work committed to thinking through Foucault's legacy to Victorian studies, work like Lauren Goodlad's *Victorian Culture and the Victorian State* (2003) and David Wayne Thomas's *Cultivating Victorians* (2004). Critics of my generation inherited a set of profoundly influential Foucauldian works that revised the way we read the Victorian novel. *The Novel and the Police* (1988), *Desire and Domestic Fiction* (1987), *Uneven Developments* (1988), and *Epistemology of the Closet* (1990) made up our diet and, as has been widely noted, we have found it difficult to do more than regurgitate their insights. "The watershed years of the late 1970s and 1980s," Erin O'Connor contends, for example, "have left a long and ugly drought in their wake. There has been no comparably major study of nineteenth-century fiction for the past ten years and the bulk of the work being done is patently derivative, devoted to recapitulating and extending ideas laid down over a decade ago, rather than continuing its tradition of innovation" (par. 6). A few exceptions stand out, such as Christopher Lane's *Burdens of Intimacy* (1999), which refuses to let Foucault upstage Freud, but by and large Victorianists keep to the script of what Adams has called the "Foucauldian melodrama" ("Recent Studies in the Nineteenth Century" 858).[8] Before I outline the book's chapters in the final section of this introduction, "Mundane Bookkeeping Matters," I hypothesize about why this might be. Why have we found Foucault so exceedingly compelling that, even as "our broadly Foucauldian preoccupation with power verges on reduction to an utterly banal formula," we seem paralyzed to transcend him? (Adams, "Recent Studies in the Nineteenth Century" 878) And what does this have to do with the question with which I began? The question that borrowed Foucault's own words on the modern infatuation with repression to ask about our strangely liberating self-loathing: why do we say with so much passion and so much resentment against our recent past, against our present, and against ourselves, that we are no better—are, in fact, worse—than everyone else?[9]

Sacrificing the Professional in Victorian Studies

> "It is a comfort to think what a rising profession I belong to."
> —Henry Sidgwick, 1874, quoted in Lubenow

> "I would not want to be a Victorian scholar these days."
> —Literature professor quoted in *Chronicle of Higher Education*, 2002

The Foucauldian essay that did the most to shape Victorian studies' approach to the figure of the professional is without question Mary Poovey's "The Man-of-Letters Hero: *David Copperfield* and the Professional Writer." This brilliant chapter from *Uneven Developments* argues that *David Copperfield* distracts readers from David's implication in the vulgar market by appropriating the disinterest associated with the self-sacrificing wife and mother. According to this view, David needs Agnes not because her selflessness complements his disinterestedness but because it throws a mystifying veil over his mercenary motives. We have been operating ever since under the assumption that the nineteenth-century professional fostered the illusion that he transcended the market upon which he exchanged his services. We charge ourselves with exposing this fraudulent claim, laying bare the rhetorical machinations behind the professional's apparent transcendence. But can it be only coincidence that demystifying the professional became an irresistible thesis at the same time a shrinking academic market put critics under unprecedented pressure to professionalize? If literary works are allegories of their own production, as some have claimed, could not literary criticism also harbor self-referential allegories? Might twinned impulses of resentment (over professionalization's acceleration) and self-abnegation (for critics' own participation) play a role in the sacrifice of the professional?

In the mid-nineteenth century, the novelist viewed herself or himself as part of the professional class s/he was helping to usher forth. In the late twentieth and early twenty-first centuries, literary critics have only begun to think of themselves as members of, as one scholar writes, "what we now call a 'profession'" (Harpham, "End of Theory" 194). "Where the word 'professional' seemed a bit off in 1950," George Levine comments, "now it would be merely absurd to deny that humanities departments are in the business of professional training" ("Aesthetics and Ideology Revisited" 4). Sociologically classified as professionals for the whole of the twentieth century, we never referred to ourselves as such but rather as "intellectuals" or "scholars" or, more recently, "teachers of critical thinking." Now we are professional academics, our colleagues are more or less "professionalized," and our graduate students are "preprofessional" or, what is more of the same thing, "hyperprofessional."[10] Adopting this identity has been fraught from the start, as is clear in the slide from the anodyne "professional" to the pathological "hyperprofessional" as well as in Levine's brutally crisp formulation, "the business of professional training."

Anxiety about "the state of the profession" has gone hand-in-hand with thinking of ourselves as professionals, and the term "profession" seems both a defense against and a metonym for crisis. That is, to identify oneself with "the profession" is to feel at once nested in an institution with a respected history *and* wildly swung among the cumulative crises threatening the profession with incoherence since the 1980s—crises ranging from, to quote one critic, "the political demonization of the NEA and the NEH, the media manufacture of a 90s red scare . . . incessant carping in the media and among humanities scholars about the fashions of cultural studies and canon revision, and any number of more local skirmishes about the value of language disciplines in general . . . to say nothing of the more pressing and troubling corporate reorganization of our universities" (Gregory, par. 1). When one invokes "the profession," one both quells anxiety and incites it.

To some scholars, the ubiquity of the term indicates our fall from the status of intellectual into reified specialist.[11] Recently Geoffrey Galt Harpham has argued that the rise of a narrow professionalism marks the end of the heady, speculative era of theory. "Fields of cultural endeavor, once heroic, now consider themselves 'Professions,'" he writes; "The rise of professionalism made literary study available not just to aesthetically responsive scholars but to ambitious people who understood the structure and ethos of a post-theoretical professionalism" ("End of Theory" 194). A whiff of blame-the-victim clings to this essay, which nowhere mentions the altered academic market forcing young literary critics to put their ambitions on hyperbolic display. Indeed, aspiring critics—graduate students—are the ones predisposed to feel the most ambivalent about professionalization. On the one hand, if professionalization is taken to mean an aggressive self-marketing achieved primarily through research productivity, one might view it as intellectual quantity at the price of quality, and this view might provide a tempting compensatory buffer when the young scholar as yet lacks quantity. On the other hand, non-productivity is not an alternative that will land the student a job and so she perforce must produce and "professionalize." A colleague who earned her PhD at Duke in the 1990s reports, "We were ironic about the professionalization of graduate programs even as we were anxious about our own professionalization. We were defensively ironic."

While the rise of the profession spells the end of theory for Harpham, the rise of theory coincides with—in fact, constitutes—criticism's professionalization for John Guillory. In his influential book *Cultural Capital* and in a series of equally influential essays since, Guillory argues that literary study, once an important form of cultural capital, is increasingly marginalized in a post-1970s economy favoring a new technical-professional class over the traditional middle class. One need not be familiar with Shakespeare to join the ranks of this new class but rather must possess certain skills. Theory's "rigor," he suggests, can be viewed as an unconscious response to this new economy, a misrecognized attempt to "model the intellectual work of the theorist on the new social form of intellectual work, the technobureaucratic labor of the new professional-managerial class" (183). In fact, Guillory's argument that new economic conditions have sidelined literature allows him to read any number of the profession's moments—from the theory explosion in the 1970s to the canon debate in the 1980s to the emergence of cultural studies and the "preprofessionalism" of graduate students in the 1990s—as symptoms of "a larger, protracted crisis in the decline of the relevance of the humanities" ("Bourdieu's Refusal" 128).

Guillory's sociological approach connecting the profession's internal changes to larger, structural changes in its social status is more promising than one that accounts for change in terms of generational temperaments. It also usefully redirects our attention from local skirmishes over, say, cultural studies to the ugly reality of our downsizing. But Guillory's fatalism is disabling.

Training our gaze on the real threat to literary study, Guillory then tells us that all we can do is sit back and watch the death throes of our cultural capital. About the global conditions determining our local circumstances in the academy, he writes, "there is nothing that members of our profession can do" ("Preprofessionalism" 5).[12] A number of critics echo Guillory.[13] Levine, for example, offers a set of recommendations to English departments in a recent article, cites Guillory, and then concludes on the following dispirited note: "In the end, what happens to the profession and to the teaching we are supposed to be doing in it is likely to be largely decided by forces well beyond the control of even the strongest energies inside higher education" ("Two Nations" 16).

Guillory's argument rests on two premises that come together to make the end of literary study as we know it a foregone conclusion. Guillory assumes that the economy has qualitatively changed since around 1970, and he is no doubt right about that (see Harvey, *Condition of Postmodernity*). In today's post-Fordist economy, intellectual labor is much more valuable but far less secure. However, Guillory's corollary assumption that literary study is irrelevant to this new economy is less obviously the case. He points to declining enrollment in literature classes since 1970 as evidence of our increasing futility, but, looking at the data on enrollment from a different angle, the question becomes not why did enrollment drop in the 1970s, but rather why has there been, as Michael Bérubé writes, "a resurgence of undergraduate interest in the English major in the 1980s and 1990s?" (*Employment of English* 21). The new economy, Bérubé persuasively argues, creates a context in which "a general liberal arts degree might be seen by prospective employers as more attractive than a degree that signified a college career of technical-vocational training" (22). "Whatever the status of 'literature' as an index of cultivation and class status," he continues, "degrees in English may still be convertible into gainful employment—*not* because they mark their recipients as literate, well-rounded young men and women who can allude to Shakespeare in business memos, but because they mark their recipients as people who can potentially negotiate a wide range of intellectual tasks and handle (in various ways) disparate kinds of 'textual' material" (23). Looked at this way, the conflict of interest is not between literature professors and the students who no longer need them, but between humanities faculty and a new administrative culture deploying the cost-cutting techniques of the new economy.[14] In other words, it is a labor relations issue—an issue for the profession *as a profession*, as a body that insists on defining for itself the terms and organization of its practice. "The historical shaping of the knowledge class," John Frow explains, "took place around a process of legal and industrial struggle over the conditions for autonomy of work practices" (125).

Ironically, then, we have begun to refer to "the profession" at precisely the moment we face deprofessionalization. Having conceded our modest identity as professionals, we find we are, again, out of step with reality—that, to borrow Bill Readings's now-famous line, "the professoriat is being proletarianized" (1). Charles B. Harris elaborates, "What we thought was the contested terrain—such issues as the literary canon, multiculturalism, the humanities curriculum—turns out to have been merely a beachhead. Now we understand that the real targets of this escalating assault are tenure and shared governance, the twin bulwarks of our professional identity" (25).[15] Although our autonomy was always relative, the institutions of shared governance and tenure ensured that it was not simply chimerical. Increasingly, universities and colleges replace retiring tenured faculty in literature departments not with tenure-line hires but with adjunct labor without the job security or work conditions that make relative autonomy possible.[16] The pre- and hyperprofessionalization of junior scholars is best understood, therefore, not as the profession's invasion by careerist critics but as the consequence of heightened competition stemming from a catch-22: dwindling demand for fresh (or stale) PhDs, as tenure lines evaporate, and an oversupply of PhDs, as departments expand graduate programs in misguided and often hapless bids to hold onto tenure lines.[17] If "disavowal" is understood psychoanalytically as the simultaneous recognition and denial of a disturbing reality, perhaps our now-incessant invocation of "the profession" is one way we disavow our deprofessionalization.

"It is only with reference to the articulations and hierarchy of a professional bureaucracy that a sense of the self and its worth—its merit—emerges and becomes measurable," Stanley Fish writes, underscoring the way the professional's sense of his unique merit is paradoxically contingent upon the collective apparatus of educational institutions and professional associations. "Everyone wants to believe," Fish continues, "that his rewards have been earned rather than bestowed, and conversely, everyone wants to believe that his ill fortune is a comment not on his abilities, but on the perversity of a corrupt and blinkered system" ("Authors-Readers" 27). During periods of professional instability and contraction, when whole armies of undeniably qualified professionals collect at the bottom of the ladder, the successful and the unsuccessful alike find it hard to believe that "rewards have been earned rather than bestowed" and that the system is not "corrupt and blinkered." "I don't believe in meritorious competition anymore," one assistant professor writes in the *Chronicle of Higher Education*; "There's so little difference between [struggling adjuncts] and me that claiming superiority would be an exercise in silliness" (Coleman C3). Self-consciousness about the mechanisms of the profession spreads, and the fact that "the self of the professional is constituted and legitimized by the very structures—social and institutional—from which it is supposedly aloof" looms into view, seeming to expose professionalism itself as inherently and irredeemably compromised (Fish, "Authors-Readers" 27). As a result, the idealistic individualizing rhetoric of "calling" is replaced with the cynical, deindividualizing rhetoric of bureaucracy—"the spirit [now] is bureaucratic rather than charismatic," Harpham writes ("End of Theory" 194)—and the only way one can conceive of escaping bureaucracy is by betraying how thoroughly one is determined by it. At such a juncture, a Foucauldianism unmasking the meritocratic ideology of liberal individualism as a disciplinary regime necessarily carries the ring of truth.

Certainly, it is the case that, as Jeff Nunokawa writes, Foucault inspired "the strain of literary criticism that has told the most on the Victorian novel over the course of the last two decades" (843). Perhaps the most exemplary of the work exploring the Victorian novel's participation in the ruses of liberal individualism remains D. A. Miller's *The Novel and the Police.* According to Miller, the Victorian novel inscribes a disciplinary double bind whereby the bourgeois individual's belief in her autonomy only conscripts her in her own incarceration. What is the relationship between a Foucauldian vision of self-defeating agency and the critic's experience of professional disequilibrium, when the critic's compensatory hyperprofessionalization accompanies the structural devaluation of the profession itself? Speaking of *David Copperfield*'s ragtag cast of characters, Miller describes a "spectacle of . . . pathetically reduced beings, maimed by their own defense mechanisms, and whose undoubtedly immense energy can only be expended to fix them all the more irremovably in a total social system" (207). Is this point particularly persuasive under conditions when the "undoubtedly immense energy" of the critic only invests her further in a rapidly depreciating discipline, a field devalued by the university and, as Guillory at least argues, the culture as a whole? However unconscious and mediated the connection, it can be no accident that it is precisely when we are experiencing a very real shrinking of our professional autonomy that we come to "realize" that autonomy itself is illusory.

Miller does not finger the professional per se, but that figure exemplifies liberal individualism. Putatively succeeding on the basis of his own merits and considered "the proprietor of his own person and capacities," the professional is the hero in the liberal fantasy of individual autonomy and, consequently, the scapegoat in the Foucauldian unmasking of liberalism (Larson 222). As if to bring this subtext to the surface, Mary Poovey's "The Man-of-Letters Hero: *David Copperfield* and the Professional Writer" appeared soon after Miller's essay on the same novel. Whereas Miller's exposé of liberalism is arguably also an implicit or displaced scandal of professionalism, Poovey's masterful piece explicitly indicts the professional. In her hands, the professional becomes both a synecdoche for and the agent of a liberalism that champions freedom but secretly defers to the market and/or disciplinary society. The professional, she writes, "reinforced and disguised" the lie of liberal individualism (107).[18]

A hermeneutics of suspicion governs Poovey's reading: David is "self-serving" (118), "manipulat[ive] (117), and "complicitous" (120), while the novel itself "collude[s]" (122), cover[s] over" (123), "distracts" (119), and "disguise[s]" (122).[19] Positing a zero-sum game wherein one ascends social and economic heights only by pushing others down, Poovey argues that the professional appears meritorious only insofar as others are understood to be undeserving.[20] The novel papers over the fact that others might be equally worthy by translating class differences into variations of moral character. This argument rides on Poovey's ability to persuade us that no qualitative difference separates David from Uriah Heep. David and Uriah "manipulate others for their self-serving ends," she writes, "[but] whereas Heep's connivances are eventually clearly revealed, David's manipulations remain obscure. Only when the reader reads against the narrator's disarming claims do certain actions appear as what they are: self-aggrandizing attempts to better himself at someone else's expense" (117).

Poovey's approach dismantles professional identity by conflating the professional with other classed identities, alternately conflating him with the capitalist and the manual laborer. When she focuses on David's hidden greed, she wants to demonstrate that the professional and the capitalist are essentially identical—both equally acquisitive and exploitative of others. And, as I argue below, when she drops the professional's dissimulated motives to consider the organization and conditions of professional work, she wishes to show that the professional and the factory hand are one and the same—both equally alienated. In sum, for Poovey, professional services are just like other commodities on the market. If we believe they are different, it is simply because Victorian novels like *David Copperfield* have convinced us so. Or did they? "The extent of symbolic work necessary to deploy these figures (literary man and domestic woman) revealed that they were not really outside the market economy or class society," writes Poovey (123). The fictive act suggesting that professional and domestic work is something other than self-interested labor has been *too* assiduously performed or, rather, the professional protests too much—his declarations of innate and earned merit betray his anxiety that he depends on the class system he allegedly transcends. But then it might just as reasonably be claimed that Poovey has had to expend a great deal of energy herself. Without Poovey, would we have believed that the literary man and the housewife were in fact qualitatively different from the market-oriented capitalist and laborer? And would we have been simply *wrong*?

Perhaps symbolic performances like *David Copperfield* did go some way toward placing professional and domestic careers in another realm and generating another logic to regulate their practice. Perhaps the experience of being a professional or housewife was different precisely because it was *believed* to be different by those having the experience. For help conceptualizing this here, and throughout *Novel Professions*, I rely on Barbara Herrnstein Smith's formulation of the "double discourse of value." "On the one hand," Smith writes, "there is the discourse of economic theory: money, commerce, technology, industry, production and consumption, workers and consumers; on the other hand, there is the aesthetic axiology: culture, art, genius, creation and appreciation, artists and connoisseurs" (127). Work conducted in the world of economics is self-interested and profit-oriented, exchanged as commodities, while the work of aesthetics is not work at all but "play." Poovey wishes to demonstrate that while literature claimed to belong to the latter, it actually inhabited the former discourse. Presenting himself as exempt from "the alienation endemic to all kinds of labor under capitalism" (13) and, thereby, promoting the false notion that "there was some boundary to the alienation of market relations" (118), the literary professional pretended to be engaged in aesthetics when in fact he was driven by economics. To underscore this point, Poovey details the myriad ways Victorian writing resembled Taylorized labor, discussing serialization's "factorylike conditions of production" and "standardization of form" (124). Conversely, she effaces the way belief in literature's status as artistic creation influenced the relationship the writer had to his or her writing. She also ignores the more material ways the scene of writing contrasted with the managed monotony of the assembly line, such as the ability to work at home with one's own "tools," to set one's own hours despite being on a schedule, to see what one conceives in one's head materialized through one's effort, and the like. In sum, in order to prove that literature belongs to the first discourse, a hermeneutics of suspicion denies all the ways in which it also belongs to the second. More to the point, it denies the very existence of the second discourse as anything but mere ideology.

What is gained by refusing professional labor its specificity is obvious:

sharp insight into the ways liberal individualism covers over the constitutive inequities of capitalist society. But something is lost, and not just for the student of Victorian culture. The hermeneutics of suspicion pervades literary criticism as a whole, shaping our approach to the professional and also to what we do as professionals—aesthetics. "Marxists, cultural materialists, poststructuralists, and deconstructive psychoanalysts, have . . . shared a hermeneutics of suspicion," Isobel Armstrong writes in *The Radical Aesthetic*, and consequently, "the concept of the aesthetic has been steadily emptied of content" (2). Like the professional, the thinking goes, aesthetics is not what it purports to be. This parallel makes perfect sense once one considers the significant overlap between discourses of aesthetics and professionalism, both of which define practitioners by their distance from economic determination.[21] In fact, the critical pillorying of the professional is best considered a subset of the last two decades' deconstruction of aesthetic autonomy—the discovery that "disinterested assessment" and "autonomy" are ideological mystifications.

While Armstrong is surely right about the general tenor of contemporary criticism, she too hastily assimilates the "Marxists" and "cultural materialists" into the group she names, forgetting that a certain strain of Marxist thinking always bore art's position within both discourses in mind.[22] Peter Bürger wrote in *The Theory of the Avant-Garde* (1984):

> Conceiving of art's apartness from society as its 'nature,' means involuntarily adopting the *l'art pour l'art* concept of art and simultaneously making it impossible to explain this apartness as the product of a historical and social development. If, on the other hand, one puts forward the view that art's independence from society exists only in the artist's imagination . . . the correct insight that autonomy is a historically conditioned phenomenon turns into its denial; what remains is a mere illusion. Both approaches miss the complexity of autonomy, whose characteristic is that it describes something real (the detachment of art as a special sphere from the nexus of the praxis of life) but simultaneously expresses this real phenomenon in concepts that block recognition of the social determinacy of the process. (36)

The aesthetic discourse in the double discourse of value cannot be reduced to "mere illusion." Certainly, this discourse fetishizes art by obscuring all the labor producing the art object that cannot be attributed to the artist's effortless "genius," but one is not at liberty to dismiss it from one's analysis on that basis alone. Art has an autonomy despite its being only "apparent" or, rather, precisely *because* it appears to.[23]

The appearance of art's autonomy is an impression built up over time, as neo-Marxist Pierre Bourdieu painstakingly illustrates in his 1996 *Rules of Art.* I will return to Poovey below, but I want to pause on Bourdieu for a moment because the logic of cultural production he outlines informs much of *Novel Professions.* It might seem strange that a book critical of the "prevailing hermeneutics of suspicion" would mobilize Bourdieu, considering that Anglo-American critics view him as an economic determinist who cynically reduces intellectual and aesthetic disinterest to self-interest (Thomas ix).[24] "The constitution of relatively autonomous areas of practice," Bourdieu writes, "is accompanied by a process through which symbolic interests (often described as 'spiritual' or 'cultural') come to be set up in opposition to strictly economic interests as defined in the field of economic transactions by the fundamental tautology 'business is business'; strictly 'cultural' or 'aesthetic' interest, disinterested interest, is the paradoxical product of the ideological labor in which writers and artists, those most directly interested, become autonomous by being opposed to material interests, i.e., by being symbolically nullified as interests" ("Structures" 172). Those persons most directly interested represent themselves as disinterested, he says, and this might be taken to imply that the artist or writer is hypocritical, or, at best, obtusely unaware of her own unconscious motivations. Bourdieu means to suggest neither. His word is "paradox"—the principle of aesthetic autonomy is the "paradoxical product" of "ideological labor." "The fundamental law of this *paradoxical* game," Bourdieu repeats in *Rules of Art,* "is that there one has an interest in disinterestedness" (21). If the artist or writer's work is to enjoy any abiding value, we must perceive it to have been produced without regard to exchange value. Disavowing the market, the artist makes one possible (though not inevitable). This is not semantics but a historically determined reality produced through the "process of autonomization of the intellectual and artistic field" that began in reaction to the emergence of market capitalism ("Field of Cultural Production" 36).[25]

This is not to say that critics have simply misread Bourdieu but that his formulations are better read in light of his larger project. Certainly *Distinction* scorns the principle of disinterestedness as inauthentic class ideology by demonstrating that the appreciation of the autotelic art object requires not an essentially superior capacity of judgment but a kind of elite training in the snobbish rewards of difficult art. And, similarly, but from the perspective of art production rather than consumption, *Rules of Art* shows how the posture of aesthetic autonomy is disingenuous in at least one sense—Flaubert could only tout his artistic independence from the commercial market, because he possessed economic independence. In *Rules of Art,* however,

Bourdieu moves beyond a hermeneutics of suspicion, yielding a dialectical advance: he argues that the principle of aesthetic and intellectual autonomy is an element of class mystification and, *at the same time*, is among the "most precious collective achievements of intellectuals" (339). Over the course of a century, intellectuals—Flaubert being the most visible—developed a critical disposition that was "simultaneously the product and the guarantee of their autonomy" (339). "Objective structures . . . become mental structures through a learning process that takes place in a universe organized according to these same structures and subject to sanctions formulated in a language also structured according to the same oppositions," explains Bourdieu (*State Nobility* 39). In a chicken-and-egg fashion, proclamations of independence facilitated the institutionalizations of independence—practices of peer review, fellowships not tied to special interests, and so on—and vice versa. By consolidating both the institutional basis for assertions of intellectual independence and a mass-cultural audience for those assertions, artists and intellectuals created a position of relative autonomy from which they could then speak about affairs of state and the market with peculiar authority (Bourdieu cites the Dreyfus affair as the first major example of this).

Critics have noticed the shift from *Distinction* to *Rules of Art* and have interpreted it as a kind of logical discrepancy or contradiction. Nicholas Brown and Imre Szeman comment, for example, "Bourdieu's work . . . seems increasingly to posit a politics and ethics on an implicit aesthetics that is apparently at odds with claims he makes at other places in his work" (5). And Allen Dunn identifies a "gap between Bourdieu's demystifying account of various social practices and the various types of value commitment evident in his calls for reform," though he acknowledges that "the tensions that shape [Bourdieu's] work may be productive as well as problematic" ("Review" 202–3). Guillory, perhaps Bourdieu's most careful reader in the United States, has articulated the difference between the texts without reducing it to contradiction. "In comparing *Distinction*'s critique of consumption with Bourdieu's description elsewhere of restricted production," he writes, "[we discover] that the severity of *Distinction*'s critique of consumption is inversely related to his idealization of autonomous production" (*Cultural Capital* 338). To what extent, Guillory implies, can this inconsistency be seen as a virtue, revealing a truth about the artist-intellectual? How is the autonomy of the artist-intellectual both an instance of class privilege and an institutionalized logic that can act as an indispensable "check" on other institutionalized forms of power?

"The disavowal [of self-interest]," Bourdieu writes, "is neither a real negation of the 'economic' interest which always haunts the most 'disinterested' practices, nor a simple 'dissimulation' of the mercenary aspects of the practice" ("Production of Belief" 262). The disavowal of self-interest might be understood as the result of a fit between "social and mental structures" (*State Nobility* 1), a disposition shaped by the professional apparatus and social world of professionalism (and art). What Bourdieu describes is not so far from Freud's understanding of sublimation as a socially valuable form of repression. Because professions require long periods of apprenticeship or knowledge acquisition, individuals must "discipline" themselves by repressing immediate desires, and thus foregoing immediate rewards, in favor of more immaterial and/or long-term goals. As sociologist Oswald Hall has written, one begins the process of becoming a professional by first "generating an ambition" and "one function of an ambition is to discipline present conduct in the interest of a future goal" (89). "An ambition," he continues, "is usually conceived to be a highly subjective matter, generated in private fashion and internalized as a drive. . . . The fewer the day-to-day rewards in the early stages of a career and the longer delayed the substantial rewards, the more ambition is needed" (89). One must become adept at repressing self-interest,. channeling desire into what Eliot in *Middlemarch* calls "far-reaching investigation" (145) and "far-resonant action" (vii). One must work up an internal drive by investing "far-reaching inquiry" with its own erotic charge, as Eliot illustrates when she explains how Lydgate happens upon his vocation:

> The page he opened on was under the heading of "Anatomy" and the first passage that drew his eyes was on the valves of the heart. He was not much acquainted with valves of any sort, but he knew that *valvae* were folding doors, and through this crevice came a sudden light startling him with his first vivid notion of finely adjusted mechanism in the human frame. A liberal education had of course left him free to read the indecent passages in the school classics, but beyond a general sense of secrecy and obscenity in connexion with his internal structure, had left his imagination quite unbiased . . . the moment of vocation had come, and before he got down from his chair the world was made new to him by a presentiment of endless processes . . . From that hour Lydgate felt the growth of an intellectual passion. (142–43)

Putting Eliot's logic in reverse, one could say that the peeping tom is the failed doctor, the man who could not generate a durable ambition out of his early excitements. (And, indeed, the first "crisis" to almost derail Lydgate is one prompted by the voyeurism of theatergoing.) This early excitement must supply ambition with enough energy to withstand the many temptations and aggravations competing for the self's attention, particularly during the long period of credentialing. In Lydgate's case, as Eliot explains, "scientific interest" must take "the form of professional enthusiasm" that is "not to be stifled by that initiation in makeshift called his 'prentice days' . . . [or] his studies in London, Edinburgh, and Paris" (143).

Disavowal is not the same as denial, it is important to remember. Whereas the latter attempts to refuse a repressed desire wholesale, the former converts part of it into something that can be admitted into consciousness. Victorian writers were quite capable of such a distinction and in Victorian fiction "disinterest" is a remarkably elaborated term that is not always, or even perhaps usually, placed in simple opposition to economic self-interest. Instead "disinterest" is often predicated upon an acknowledgment of self-interest. Characters who have trouble admitting to themselves all the ways in which they are beholden to their own desires are the least "independent" of Victorian characters—denial being the defense mechanism of the hypocrite, like *Middlemarch*'s Mr. Bulstrode. Conversely, Bulstrode's counterpoint Mr. Farebrother is perhaps the most magnanimous character in all of Victorian fiction and one who can freely admit, for example, that he covets a particular post not for the souls he can save but because he "should be glad of the forty pounds" (174). Victorian authors already knew, that is to say, what Bourdieu figures out in *Rules of Art*—that "disinterest" cannot be pure self-sacrifice without turning into mere dissimulation but that the options are not purity versus complicity in the first place.[26] "Intellectuals are paradoxical beings who cannot be thought of as such as long as they are apprehended through the obligatory alternative between autonomy and commitment, between pure culture and politics," he writes (340).[27] Rather, autonomy makes politics possible as anything more than the private opinion of an individual. What results from disavowal, then, is neither absolute freedom nor deferred capitulation to special interests but rather "the freedom of the *salon des refuses*, who reject those who reject them and who establish an antithetical market in symbolic goods," as Guillory writes of the artists. "The point is not, then," he continues, "simply to expose this freedom as unreal, when in fact the space cleared by the refusal of market demand is precisely the space in which social determinations can be explored without wholly acceding to market demand and in which many new possibilities for the development of art are created" ("Bourdieu's Refusal" 394). The surprisingly self-scrutinized Victorian professional might be a model, then, for our own activity as intellectuals. In particular, such a figure might encourage us to recognize that the "crisis of the profession" is not a crisis of too much professionalization, as it is often portrayed, but of too little—an erosion of professional control over the autonomous work practices that are simultaneously the guarantee of and the reward for our interested disinterestedness. (The rewards we experience as professionals are directly tied to our autonomy. In a survey of professors, Judith Gappa and Shelly MacDermid found that by far "the greatest level of satisfaction [86 percent] came from faculty autonomy and independence" [5].)

To return to Poovey, I hope it is now clear that by unmasking aesthetic "freedom" Poovey unravels the paradox whereby certain kinds of work are not understood as *work* but only at the high cost of sacrificing what is unique about professional labor. Poovey complains that Dickens's depiction of David's writing and Agnes's housekeeping "convey[s] the twin impressions that some kinds of work are less 'degrading' and less alienating than others and that some laborers are so selfless and skilled that to them work is simultaneously an expression of self and a gift to others" (101). If one agrees with Poovey that the logic of market relations informs every pursuit in one way or another, does that necessarily mean all labor is equally alienated? Is writing a story the same as capping bottles? Can work never gratify the self while also doubling as a gift to others? "In the experience of vocation," writes Mintz, "selfish ambitions for personal distinction and selfless aspirations toward general amelioration are parts of a single matrix of desire" (20). Relatively autonomous cultural production does not rely primarily upon individual exceptionalism but is built into institutions and dispositions over the course of a century. And the vocational disposition, in circular fashion, depended on the development of institutions organized so as to cultivate in its members a pleasure in holding the market at arm's length.

All work under capitalism is certainly implicated in capitalism's logic of equivalence, but that does not mean all work is equal. Hunting down the gaps, contradictions, and subterfuges of a text, a hermeneutics of suspicion is incapable of withholding judgment in order to illuminate the positive as well as the negative aspects of professionalism. "The dialectic's first function," Fredric Jameson writes, "[is] the suspension of the moralizing judgment, the transcendence of good and evil, which is to say, the neutralization of some choice between the positive and the negative judgment" ("Theoretical Hesitation" 277). Denouncing the professional, Victorianists fail to see that this figure's paradoxical position inside and outside the market—at once complicit and transcendent—is not a counterfeit but a dialectic—that is, a position that works both ways, enabling but also destabilizing the system within which it functions. The professions enable capitalism by falsely holding out the promise of unalienated labor to everyone. Yet they also destabilize it because by holding out the promise of gratifying work, they remind us that work should be gratifying. The professions, as Herbert Marcuse wrote in *Negations* about art, contain "not only quiescence about what is, but also remembrance of what could be" (98).

Mundane Bookkeeping Matters

> When I think of the future of literary studies, I try to concentrate . . . on the mundane bookkeeping matters of the profession, out of the conviction that if the profession offers its aspirants good material and intellectual working conditions, the shape and the range of the knowledges produced in the profession will eventually take care of themselves.
> —Michael Bérubé ("Days of Future Past" 20)

"Isn't there, after all (and risking accusations of naiveté), something pretty decent and creative in a struggle to get beyond the self?" George Levine asks in his latest study of the Victorians, *Dying to Know* (2002), which he characterizes as "something of a defense of those impossible strivings toward disinterest" (14, 13). "Is it true," he wonders, "that all disinterest is interested?" (14). However close my thesis may appear to his, I would argue that any defense of "disinterest" must first recognize that it requires the advocacy of one's self-interest. Second, it must acknowledge the fact that "disinterest" no longer has the cultural resonance it once enjoyed. Whereas Bourdieu traces the nineteenth-century construction of the high/mass culture boundary, a boundary intimately tied up with the disinterest/interest dualism, Paul DiMaggio describes its contemporary erosion: "Changes in social structure and the rise of an open market of cultural goods have weakened institutionalized cultural authority, set off spirals of cultural inflation, and created more differentiated, less hierarchical, less universal, and less symbolically potent systems of cultural classification than those in place during the first part of this century" (39). As a result of these complex changes, the principle of disinterestedness, once critical to the legitimation of professional identity, has lost some of its rhetorical edge. But even if it were still effective, the ideal of disinterest may actually work against professionals now, at least those in academia. As Andrew Ross argues, the ideal cultivates in scholars a capacity for self-sacrifice that has been used to deprive them of their work autonomy by "ma[king] it easy for power to shift rapidly to managers and administrators" ("Mental Labor Problem" 23). Faculty must insist rather on their "autonomy," a term only a short metonymic distance from "disinterest," but one more likely to resonate with both a professoriate and a public suspicious of claims to purity.

"It's in vain, Trot, to recall the past, unless it works some influence upon the present," Aunt Betsey says to David Copperfield, and this book is motivated in part by concern over the structural declassing of today's professional (329). As numerous professions devolve into managed labor, it is hard to remember that historically professions have been defined by "the degree to which they . . . gained the organized power to control themselves the terms, conditions and content of their work in the settings where they perform their work" (Friedson 22). There is a disorienting disconnect between pundits' representation of intellectual labor and its lived experience. We are bombarded with jingoism about living in the so-called Information Age, "the domination of intellectual over manual labor" (Aronowitz, "On Intellectuals" 52), the skyrocketing importance of immaterial labor (Hardt), the need for symbolic analysts in a global economy (Reich), "expertise call[ing] the tune in today's economic order" (Hodges xii), and "the rise of a creative class" (Florida), while at the same time tremendous job insecurity exists among the well-credentialed, management places ever-greater pressure on knowledge workers to produce more surplus value, and a crushing gap exists between the intellectual skills possessed and the formulaic work increasingly required. It has become more difficult to maintain that professionals "enjoy a semi-autonomy that gives [them] a freedom in their work afforded no other laborers in today's economy" (McGowan 44). Certainly, it is hard to maintain this with regard to academics when, as Gary Rhoades demonstrates in *Managed Professionals*, "the terms and position of faculty's professional labor are being renegotiated as managers seek to reform, reinvent, re-engineer, redesign, or reorganize colleges and universities" (2).

At a time when nonacademic journals like *Salon* run pieces entitled "From Ivory Tower to Academic Sweatshop" (Wright), it comes as something of a shock to stumble across the following sentence in *The Political Unconscious*: "It is surely fatuous," Jameson wrote in 1981, "for intellectuals to seek to glamorize their tasks—which can for the most part be subsumed under the rubric of the elaboration, reproduction, or critique of ideology—by assimilating them to real work on the assembly line and to the experience of the resistance of matter in genuine labor" (45).[28] That any professor working today would think comparing her tasks to a factory job glamorizes them would be funny if it were not so ironic.[29] The factory may have been the vehicle of benign, and even romantic, metaphors as late as 1981, but it is now all too literal, as new titles on education's corporate reorganization seek to make clear—titles such as Stanley Aronowitz's *The Knowledge Factory: Dismantling the Corporate University and Creating True Higher Learning* (2001), David F. Noble's *Digital Diploma Mills: The Automation of Higher Education* (2002), and Deborah Herman and Julie Schmid's *Cogs in the Classroom Factory: The Changing Identity of Academic Labor* (2003).

Jameson implies that the key distinction is that which separates brainwork from handiwork—"writing and thinking" from hammering and hauling. "One cannot assimilate without intellectual dishonesty the 'production' of texts to the production of goods by factory workers: writing and thinking are not alienated labor in that sense," he writes (45). But the key difference between alienated and unalienated labor, as Harry Braverman argued three decades ago, is rather the discrepancy between the experience of work that unites conception and execution and the experience of work that parcels them out. Prying conception and execution apart has the effect of separating means from ends and turning the means into what Jameson elsewhere has called "desacralized technique" ("Vanishing Mediator" 8). Creative work, however, produces "objects that [figuratively] 'return' to their creator, thereby permitting the entire 'reappropriation' of one's own activity" (Moretti 116).[30] Opposed to the monotonously repeated task undertaken without any conception of the process as a whole, it is the gratifying loop that begins as an idea in one's head, becomes a reality through one's creative efforts, and is now reflected upon in the outside world.

I propose that we reserve "professional" to designate those efforts performed under the relatively autonomous conditions that foster creativity. My intent is not to restrict creative labor to the traditionally defined professions—law, medicine, and so on—but to universalize an idea associated with the professions. The association of creative labor with the professions can be found throughout the nineteenth and twentieth centuries. When H. Byerley Thomson attempted to differentiate professional labor from other gainful employment in his 1857 *The Choice of a Profession*, he used artistic labor to characterize professional labor as a whole:

> The test by which an operation belongs to intellectual, or to bodily labour, or to barter is by observing what is the *principal object* of the exertion. Thus an artist sells to his client a certain quantity of canvas, covered with a thick coat of paint, the whole surrounded by a gilt frame; but he is not therefore a merchant, the principal object, and real consideration of the purchase being the intellectual, and imaginative design expressed by the picture, to which point canvas, and frame are subordinate accessories. (3)

At the moment Thomson defined professional labor, it was the artist and not the more predictable lawyer or the doctor that stood as the paradigmatic professional. Over a century later, in 1971, when D.W. Winnicott wanted to suggest the diversity of the "creative impulse," he wrote, "[the creative impulse] is present as much in the moment-by-moment living of a backward child who is enjoying breathing as it is in the inspiration of an architect who suddenly knows what it is that he wishes to construct, and who is thinking in terms of material that can actually be used so that his creative impulse may take form and shape, and the world may witness" (69). In order to portray creativity's range, Winnicott established a continuum between an example that virtually nobody would recognize as creative—breathing—and an example that presumably everybody would recognize as creative—the thought process of an architect. It is no accident that when Winnicott wanted to invoke archetypal creative work, the work he chose belonged to the category "professional."

Admittedly, the reverse is also true: for the same duration of time, the professional has been associated with soul-stultifying bureaucracy. "I scarcely know a professional man I can like," wrote the narrator of J. A. Froude's 1849 *The Nemesis of Faith*: "You know a lawyer when you see him, or a doctor, or a professional clergyman. They are not simply men, but men of a particular sort, and, unfortunately, something not more but less than men—men who have sacrificed their own selves to become the paid instruments of a system" (2–3). And when, in 1923, Georg Lukács developed the concept of "reification," it was the professional not the proletariat who exemplified its extreme case: "The problems of consciousness arising from wage labour were repeated in the ruling class in a refined and spiritualized, but, for that very reason, intensified form. . . . The journalist's lack of conviction, the prostitution of his experiences and beliefs, is comprehensible only as the apogee of capitalist reification" (100). The very things that can make a professional career inspiring—working with ideas and people rather than manufacturing things—make it horrific when instrumentalized. Reproducing history's Jekyll/Hyde oscillation between the self-actualizing and the self-exploiting expert, Victorian studies cycles between affirmation and denunciation of the professional.

In *Novel Professions*, I argue that three mid-nineteenth-century novels—Charlotte Brontë's *The Professor* (1847), Charles Dickens's *David Copperfield* (1849–50), and Anthony Trollope's *The Three Clerks* (1857)—offer us an opportunity to break out of this oscillation and revise our approach to the professional. They are all narratives of professionalization that dissolved conceptual obstacles to the mid-Victorian formation of a discrete professional identity. Written during the "mid-century consolidation" of the professional ethos, they offer a series of blueprints for the professional (Reader 59).

Furthermore, two of these novels—*The Professor* and *The Three Clerks*—prove particularly resistant to a hermeneutics of suspicion, which explains in part why critics have studiously ignored them for the last twenty years. Criticism's suspicion of the professional needs him to assert a disinterest that the critic can reveal as self-interest, but neither *The Professor* nor *The Three Clerks* has its protagonist make such a claim: the former does not attempt to disingenuously distance its protoprofessional from the market but rather inserts him into it, and the latter prizes not the alleged purity of its hero but rather his impurity, his very self-interest making him a credible professional. The third text—*David Copperfield*—is the ur-object of a hermeneutics of suspicion but I argue that it produces its professional by a logic quite different from the nefarious one ascribed to it. In my view, rather than appropriating the housewife's disinterest to authorize himself, David combines the categories of capital and labor to create himself as a trustworthy professional whose talent follows the reliable routines of clock time. My readings of these novels show that when we stop scanning texts for the hypocritical gesture of disinterest we have been trained to expose, we make possible a very different critical relationship. When we withhold what Jameson called above "our moralizing judgment," we do not seize on the gap or contradiction that putatively belies the Victorian novel's version of professionalism but rather enter into its struggle to theorize intellectual labor.

Opening up our now-narrow theoretical framework, we also satisfy a historicist desire to recover the novel's role in the production of a specifically professional identity. "This book," begins another study of the Victorians, Anita Levy's *Reproductive Urges* (1999), "is occasioned by an uneasiness, become more urgent of late, with the interpretive procedures governing Victorian studies since about 1980" (1). Here, Levy speaks for many Victorianists, and I wonder if our uneasiness is related in a symptomatic way to the fact that Victorian studies uncannily, if unwittingly, reproduces the tendency of today's economy to evacuate professional identity. The contemporary economy converts professionals into knowledge workers, while the trend in Victorian studies has been to assimilate the professional into the bourgeois. Victorianists, as Pam Morris writes, "work within a monolithic model of the middle class" (679), and, thereby, Lauren Goodlad adds, obscure the "under-recognized sites of contest *within* mainstream ideologies of middle-class Englishness" (143). Both Morris and Goodlad blame this on the dominance of the Foucauldian paradigm. Criticism suffers from "an insufficiently expansive model of Victorian middle-class identity," Goodlad writes, "[for] reasons relating at least partly to the totalizing tendencies of Foucault's model of the rise of disciplinary subjectivity" (143).[31]

It has been so easy to lump the professional in with the middle class more generally in part because the emergent Victorian professional's own self-perception, as mediated by fiction, relied upon categories derived from bourgeois political economy. The Victorian novel combined the existing terms in strategic, rhetorical formulations meant to yield something altogether new. By rewriting the available plots of production with characters' "capital" (industrial or financial) and "labor" (factory, rural, or artisanal), the novel invented formulas for the value of professional services, formulas whose combinations also entailed cancellations. For example, *David Copperfield* invents professional value by combining capital and labor in such a way that the magic of capital marries the honesty of labor and, thereby, cancels capital's suspicious speculativeness and labor's machinelike monotony. Thus far, criticism has been preoccupied with how the Victorian novel produced the expert by appropriating the disinterested personas of the housewife and the aristocrat. But when free from the need to uncover disinterest's inevitable contamination by interest, we see that the novel necessarily produced the professional by first reconfiguring the market-oriented identities of the capitalist and the laborer. These novels articulate their professionals' relationship to the market by carefully building on already existing market logic.

"These 'new' middle classes," Immanuel Wallerstein has written, "were very difficult to describe in the nineteenth-century categories of analysis" (141), and even as the novels in *Novel Professions* successfully resolve ideological obstacles to professional identity formation, their attempts to draw on extant plots of labor and capital generate some telling paradoxes or structural failures: *The Professor* offers two definitions of the professional but one undercuts the other, *David Copperfield* ushers in the autonomous professional by paradoxically submitting him to the clock time associated with managed labor, and *The Three Clerks* transforms a thoughtless youth into a prosperous professional but has to give him not one but two professions to do so. Yet when we stop looking for a disavowal of self-interest—a disavowal we would be hard-pressed to find in at least two of the three novels—we view these "flaws" less as the contradictions or missteps that betray professionalism than as the inevitable by-products of attempts to define an identity that is relatively unique in the modern world—an identity that cannot be fully explained in either the terms of Adam Smith's market or Foucault's disciplinary society.

Each chapter of *Novel Professions* reads one mid-nineteenth-century novel in order to reveal the Victorians' surprisingly modern conception of an interested professionalism. Chapter 1 "Between Labor and Capital: Charlotte Brontë's *The Professor*" argues that a tension runs through the novel between representing the professional in terms of his innate mental capital and representing him in terms of his productive labor. Both representations illuminate the previously invisible—the one by seeming to materialize the immaterial mind, the other by uncovering hidden mental work—but the depiction of intellectual capacity as a timeless, natural property threatens to erase the time required for its display as labor. The final section argues that *The Professor* relies on the notion of mental capital because it imagines that such a concept works as a prophylactic against proletarianization. But mental labor is always vulnerable to being modeled upon routinized manual labor, as increasing numbers of humanities PhDs find today when they look for tenure-track salaries only to encounter a system more willing to pay them piecemeal. *The Professor's* structural failure, then, suggests that the important distinction is not between mental and manual work but rather between work that unites conception and execution and work that parcels them out.

David Copperfield solves the problem of *The Professor's* conflicting models of the professional—as mental laborer and as mental capitalist—by inventing "cultural capital," a form of capital that combines the merit of effort with the prestige of innate property. Chapter 2 "Becoming Professional: Time in *David Copperfield*" begins by surveying the post-Poovey, post-Miller field of *Copperfield* criticism. I then read *David Copperfield* as a novel authorizing the new professional class by developing a formula for professional value that relied on a mystified notion of inherent merit but which also established a standard of time discipline that required professionals to subordinate their own interests to the service of others. Broadly put, Dickens combines the finance capitalist and the factory laborer to form David Copperfield, a professional author who possesses mental capital but who, rather than speculating on it, adheres to the clock time of the patiently earned hourly wage. It is a commonplace of Dickens studies that Dickens despised factory conditions, but, as this chapter shows, he can reassure his readers that David is an honest professional only by clinging to factory time.

Like Brontë and Dickens, Trollope builds a professional in *The Three Clerks* (1857), but his professional eschews the category of capital altogether, relying solely on that of labor. Refusing the paradox of the professional established by the mid-nineteenth-century debate over competitive examinations, Trollope argues that only if the professional understands his labor as being traded for market value, not as invaluable or as removed from the taint of exchange, will he achieve relative autonomy or independence. In "The Professional Paradox: Competitive Examinations and Trollope's *The Three Clerks*" (chapter 3), I argue that this only apparently paradoxical logic chimes remarkably well with Pierre Bourdieu's thesis that disinterest is a function of institutional structures, not moral character. The last section of the chapter explains how the novel addresses the circumstances of Trollope's own highly heteronomous position in the literary marketplace in such a way that his overt self-interest as an author is "forgiven." By depicting himself in his *Autobiography* and his hero in *The Three Clerks* as a hack but doing so as if the term were one he self-reflexively embraced rather than had thrust upon him, Trollope escapes being reduced to a hack by posterity. Critics have begun, in fact, to speak of Trollope as a kind of hero. When one considers that this generation of Victorianists has been trained to read the disavowal of interest as deeply disingenuous if not downright devious, Trollope's rejection of this disavowal makes his sudden rise in critical fortune predictable.

The book's concluding chapter, "Deprofessionalized Critics in the Twenty-First Century," juxtaposes a work representative of 1990s criticism, Martha Woodmansee's *The Author, Art, and the Market* (1994), to an influential new work that is its mirror opposite, Amanda Anderson's *The Powers of Distance* (2001), in order to show that literary critics cycle predictably between exposing aesthetic value's "concealed" exchange value and reasserting aesthetic disinterest. This circuit inflicts new damage in the current context of academic deprofessionalization. Specifically, it predisposes critics to uphold a static ideological binary between self-interest and disinterest that was better suited to an earlier mode of mass production, an opposition that relies on a high/low aesthetic opposition which is itself unraveling. I argue that Victorian studies scholars today must grapple with the problems and promises of the professional not by shuttling between narratives of complicity and transcendence but rather by attending to the uniqueness of the professional's structural position—a position of relative autonomy that was a century in the making but is in jeopardy today.

A scene from *Middlemarch* perhaps best illustrates the wide divide separating autonomous intellectual labor from other forms of labor under capitalism and is, thus, a fitting scene with which to end my introduction. That archetypal professional Tertius Lydgate studies a book on fever "far into the smallest hour" by his fireside:

> As he threw down his book, stretched his legs towards the embers in the grate, and clasped his hands at the back of his head, in that agreeable afterglow of excitement when thought lapses from examination of a specific object into a suffusive sense of its connexions with the rest of our existence—seems, as it were, to throw itself on its back after strength—Lydgate felt a triumphant delight in his studies and something like pity for those less lucky men who were not of his profession. (163)

Poovey criticizes the idea that there exists a "sphere to which one can retreat—a literal or imaginative hearth . . . where one's motives do not appear as something other than what they are because self-interest and self-denial really are the same" (122). Yet in his late-night hunt for the "obscure conditions" causing fever, Lydgate does manage to gratify his *amour-propre* while simultaneously serving humanity. Savoring a literal *and* an imaginative hearth in the "agreeable afterglow" of his research, Lydgate experiences his profession as an intellectual adventure, something calling for a kind of self-denying work that doubles as self-interested play.[32] This feeling was in fact endemic to Victorians who saw themselves as part of emerging professions. Being a professional in the mid-Victorian period was, W. C. Lubenow writes, "exhilarating" (6). "It is a comfort to think what a rising profession I belong to," Henry Sidgwick wrote in a letter; one "feels at the centre of things" (qtd. in Lubenow 6).

Lydgate's transcendent moment—a "suffusive sense" of totality, "[when thought] seems, as it were, to throw itself on its back after strength"—marks the difference between, as Habermas puts it, "an objectification of essential powers and their alienation, between a satisfied praxis that returns to itself and a praxis that is impeded and fragmented" (64). It is a moment, Eliot's narrator implies, we have all felt (not specific to Lydgate, it is rather "*that* afterglow"). But while the narrator pulls us within the realm of its possibility, Lydgate kicks us out: "Lydgate felt . . . something like pity for those less lucky men who were not of his profession." Arguably, this sentence seals Lydgate's fate. Pitying others their lack of transcendent moments, he will be made by the novel to forfeit them himself. And yet, if his "something like pity" looks a little like condescension, is it not also honest? After all, most tasks do not boast that boomerang whereby thought opens out onto the world and returns to itself refreshed. For his candor—or, at the very least, for the complacency with which he assumes that he, if not his profession, will be different from "the multitude of middle-aged men who go about their vocations in a daily course determined for them much in the same way as the tie of their cravats"—Eliot condemns Lydgate to a life void of the very thing she values most—glimpses of the social totality (143). That an author so resolutely intellectual herself sacrifices her novel's intellectual is less hypocritical of Eliot than it is self-abnegating.

"We are rescued from fragmentation only by consciousness of the whole and intellectuals specialize in this consciousness," Durkheim wrote (x). In a culture in which the intellectual's very *raison d'être* is everyone else's exclusion from those moments of "consciousness of the whole" she enjoys, her self-loathing is virtually inevitable. Add to this a situation like the one facing the professional critic today, in which not only everyone else but also most of her colleagues are locked out of such moments, and her self-loathing is overdetermined.[33] Perhaps if we cease hating ourselves for being "professionals," we will be better readers of Victorian novels of professionalization. We might find, then, that the knots in their narratives do not indicate the hypocrisy of their protagonists but rather the uncanny capacity of professionalism to jam the otherwise seamless logic of modernity.

Chapter One

Between Labor and Capital:

Charlotte Brontë's The Professor

> Art works are ideological because they *a priori* posit a spiritual entity as though it were independent of any conditions of material production, hence as though it were intrinsically superior to these conditions. In so doing art works cover up the age-old culpability that lies in the divorce of physical from mental labour.
>
> —Adorno, *Aesthetic Theory*

At once outside the market and within it, the nineteenth-century professional juggled a kind of paradox. Most influential rise-of-the-professional narratives explain how the modern professional transcended the market by taking on an aura of disinterest. The professional, one version goes, reworked the aristocrat's noblesse oblige into the professional ideal of service. In another, he aligned himself with the unwaged work of the home so that he can draw on the middle-class angel's stock of self-sacrificing purity. Explaining how the professional enacted his distance from the market, both narratives assume that his proximity to the market requires no interpretation.[1] This chapter reverses that assumption. It considers a moment in the emergence of the professional class when it was not the damning presence but the apparent absence of the market that posed the dilemma. In that case, neither the aristocrat nor the middle-class angel had any rhetorical tips to offer. In the 1840s, when Charlotte Brontë wrote *The Professor*, the relative invisibility of certain kinds of work as valuable labor threatened to shut its producers out of the marketplace. Studying this novel, in which the protagonist wishes to uncover rather than cover over the price of his intellectual labor, helps correct the balance of critical studies of professionalism. In so doing, it allows us to understand these opposing directions (away from, toward the market) not only as the contradiction or the paradox of professionalism but also as its dialectic, its ability simultaneously to enable and critique the economic system in which it so ambivalently figures.

"How can a man put a price on his mind?" Silas Wegg asks rhetorically (and disingenuously) in *Our Mutual Friend* (1865), a novel that laments the market's ever-expanding reach. Written in 1846, almost two decades before Dickens's novel, Brontë's *The Professor* asks a similar question, but one that demands an answer, which takes the form of the story that unfolds. "Carry your intellect and refinement to the market and tell me in a private note what price is bid for them," a character taunts the protagonist, thereby setting the novel in motion (70). Securing a teaching position and succeeding so well that, by novel's end, he and his wife have opened their own school, the eponymous professor does indeed place his intellect on the market and, finding himself well-rewarded, has the last laugh. *The Professor*, in other words, does the opposite of what later novels like *Our Mutual Friend* train us to expect: rather than bemoan the commodification of minds, it worries about the mind's resistance to exchange value.

The difference between the two novels is an index of how far the professional class had come by 1865. By the time *Our Mutual Friend* appeared, the professional class had so clearly differentiated itself from the capitalist class that Matthew Arnold could write of "a professional class . . . with fine and governing qualities" and "an immense business class . . . without governing qualities" (qtd. in Reader 113). "By 1860," wrote Reader, "the elements of professional standing were tolerably clear" (71), and the structural contradiction of the professional—simultaneously inside and outside the market—had been papered over. *The Professor*, however, was part of an earlier moment. "In the formative period, most of the markets for professional services had to be created," Magali Larson explains, "[and] common standards of what this unique commodity—intangible services—meant . . . were lacking" (14). The problem that faced this nascent class marketing intangible services was that it had to write itself into being at least in part by representing itself in the idiom of production. It had to make mental labor visible as productive labor. However, this necessary step threatened to make the class simply another working class rather than a new kind of middle class. To prevent this possibility, the professional transformed "a service into an income-yielding property" (Perkin 7), presenting his skills as a species of innate capital or embodied property. Representing his services as simultaneously intellectual labor and intellectual capital or property, the professional conferred upon himself the merit of work and the prestige of ability, but he wrote himself as a kind of contradiction in terms.[2]

After an initial struggle, the novel's professor finds—or creates—the right market for his talent. *The Professor* itself was not so lucky: publishers rejected it nine times during Brontë's lifetime. Writing in 1851 to the publisher George Smith, Brontë joked:

> *The Professor*'s merits, I plainly perceive, will never be owned by anybody but Mr. Williams and me; very particular and unique must be our penetration, and I think highly of us both accordingly. You may allege that that merit is not visible to the naked eye. Granted; but the smaller the commodity the more inestimable its value. (Wise 3: 207)

Brontë slyly summed up the point of *The Professor*: that which appears to lack value because it is intangible ("not visible to the naked eye") is in fact more valuable. The error lies not with the commodity but with the inadequacy of conventional standards of measurement.

Reversing her strategy, this time maximizing *The Professor*'s value not by paradoxically emphasizing its smallness but by granting it heft, Brontë wrote in another letter that *The Professor* "contains . . . more substance . . . than much of *Jane Eyre*, [because] it gives, I think, a new view of a grade, an occupation" (Wise 2: 161).[3] What Brontë strove to make visible is a class that defies inherited categories of representation. She did so, first, by representing that class in terms of intellectual labor, as productive work rather than leisured play, and, second, by depicting professional expertise in terms of capital with capital's appearance of effortlessness or what Fredric Jameson calls "profit without production" (*Cultural Turn* 136). The result is an unresolved tension between labor and capital that is symptomatic of the discourse of professionalism as a whole (both then and now). Under certain circumstances, this tension can be strategic (see chapter 3 on *David Copperfield*) but in the case of *The Professor* it seems to amount, when all is said and done, to rhetorical failure.

In what follows, I outline the ideological obstacles that faced Brontë—namely, an aesthetic principle of play that repressed intellectual labor and the reduction by political economists of labor to its simplest, manual form. On the one hand, Brontë predicated professional autonomy on a critique of aesthetic autonomy that reveals its hidden labor. Resolving the problem political economy poses, on the other hand, Brontë distinguished mental work from manual labor by drawing on a phrenological discourse in which intellectual ability is figured as a form of cerebral capital. The latter strategy, however, has the effect of undercutting the former; that is to say, the emphasis on innate capital intended to rescue professional labor from proletarianization cuts against the emphasis on labor that drove Brontë's critique of aesthetics. Designed to reach the same end—professional value—but by two necessarily different routes, one strategy waylays the other. In a final section, I argue that Brontë's need to create a market for intellectual labor led her to produce a professional who inadvertently makes us reevaluate our own critical suspicion of "disinterest," a suspicion implicit in those analyses that expose the professional's attempts to disassociate himself from the market. By its very negation in her professional, we come to realize that the ideal of intellectual and aesthetic disinterest is not merely ideology, for in its desire for a realm outside the market logic of exchange it keeps alive our most humane desires.

I

To find a market for its protagonist's skills, Brontë's novel must counteract two forces conspiring to efface intellectual labor as labor: aesthetic's principle of play and political economy's definition of labor. In his account of what he calls the "separation at birth" of political economy and aesthetics, John Guillory offers two emblematic moments: Adam Smith's inability to account for consumption when determining a commodity's exchange value and Immanuel Kant's attempt to distinguish art from the commodity by rewriting the labor of art as play. While in his earlier writings, Smith argued that the commodity's beauty balanced production and consumption, beauty could not explain exchange value. Guillory writes, "[Commodities'] surplus of beauty over use failed to yield a formula for the determination of their price, their exchange value. In order to arrive at a quantum for the latter value, Smith and his contemporaries were forced to shift their analysis to the terrain of production, and thus to account for the exchange value of a commodity by reference to the quantum of labor it embodied" (*Cultural Capital* 314). Banished from political economy, the concept of beauty migrated to aesthetics where that banishment became one of its most salient characteristics. If labor (or, in Smith's phrase, "the cost of production") accounts for the commodity's value, then the absence of labor defines aesthetic value. Opposed to work undertaken for compensation, Kant's "purposiveness without purpose" is purposiveness in play. "The work of art," Guillory explains, "never quite loses the stigma of the 'compulsory,' and can only efface that stigma and distinguish itself from the commodity if its production is 'removed from all constraint, and . . . change[d] from . . . work into mere play'" (*Cultural Capital* 318).[4] Once the scene of labor is removed, art most resembles the apparently effortless productions of nature.

The discrimination of beauty is annexed to aesthetics and along with it come other forms of discrimination not primarily aesthetic but intellectual. Discrimination, as Edmund Burke defined it, for example, is comprised of both differentiation, the ability to distinguish objects from each other on the basis of their features, and evaluation, the ranking of different objects according to some principle.[5] Moral and aesthetic judgments become the province of the disinterested man of arts and letters whom Brontë called the man of "intellect and refinement"—a figure diametrically opposed to the man coarsened by trade. And, as with the work of art, the work of the discriminating intellect must be seen not as a form of work at all but as a form of play, free meditation rather than rationalized production. Honed by the Romantics, reappearing in Matthew Arnold as "disinterestedness" (246), and reaching its apotheosis in 1890s art for art's sake and, on the intellectual side, in Thorstein Veblen's prescriptive notion of "idle curiosity" ("The Place of Science in Modern Civilization"), this version of autonomy as possible only in the realm of non-utility was marshaled to distinguish certain forms of representation from the commodity throughout the nineteenth century.

Aesthetics might not have rendered intellectual pursuits "free play" in quite the way it did had political economy not modeled its concept of labor on factory labor—on, that is, direct, manual labor. Simple, objectified labor provided political economy with its needed universal equivalent. At the same moment, then, as political economy articulated its labor theory of value in such a way that only certain forms of labor qualified as labor, aesthetics predicated intellectual labor's value on its not being viewed as labor. Intellectual labor was doubly barred from the market. But even as economists, including Marx, developed their labor theory of value by eliding the intellectual work of judgment and discrimination, a rapidly changing economy was rendering that theory obsolete.[6] As Antonio Negri writes, "in the passage from manufacturing to large-scale industry . . . labor—as it became more highly qualified and complex, both individually and collectively—could not be reduced to simple, calculable quantities" (78). Intellectual labor, in short, had become a kind of oxymoron at just the moment it began to matter most.

II

In *The Professor*, Brontë proposed to write a novel in which, as she says in her preface, a "hero should work his way through life as I had seen real living men work theirs—that he should never get a shilling he had not earned." She then outfits that hero with precisely those qualities—"intellect and refinement"—

that resist quantification, making them literally invaluable (37). *The Professor* is the story of this man's quest to turn these qualities into marketable property. His quest begins as a story about two brothers virtually separated at birth—William and Edward Crimsworth—a separation that reproduces, in fact, the separation at birth of political economy and aesthetics. Orphaned and separated after the second brother's birth, the brothers have not seen each other in a decade when the novel opens. Each brother is aligned with one parent, possessing all the attributes that classed alignment suggests: the protagonist and narrator William has his aristocratic mother's physical features, creative talents, and refined sensibility while Edward looks like his capitalist father and, by the time the narrative begins, has established himself as a shrewd entrepreneur. Williams's repeated artistic metaphors and his references to his "love of an excellent or beautiful object, whether in animate or in inanimate nature" present him, at least at first, as a Romantic artist (39). At the outset, then, the novel offers an unsurprising opposition between the businessman and the aristocratic artist (the aristocrat's independence from the market reinforcing the artist's repudiation of it), but it quickly complicates this predictable opposition. William rejects an aristocratic uncle's offer to provide him with a livelihood, refusing the kind of familial obligation and dependence such an arrangement would suggest and determining instead to join his brother in trade. But just as art liberated itself from aristocratic patronage in the seventeenth and eighteenth centuries only to subject itself to the impersonal forces of the market, William realizes in retrospect that in refusing patronage to embrace commerce, he has exchanged one master for another: "I find that I was quite right to shake off the burden of patronage, but a fool to offer my shoulders instantly for the reception of another burden" (40).[7]

Translating foreign business correspondence in the countinghouse of his brother's mill, William finds that in the factory logic that organizes political economy, mental labor looks just like manual labor. "Ninety pounds a year are good wages, and I expect to have the full value of my money out of you," his brother tells him (51). That value is achieved by conditions in which the creative work of translation comes to look like the mechanical act of copying, as William describes his day to himself: "Letter-copying till noon, solitary dinner at your lodgings, letter-copying till evening, solitude" (71). De-graded to the level of the factory hand, William "endured in silence the rust and cramp of [his] best faculties" (62). The aesthetic tradition deplored just this fragmentation of the human in the division of labor, arguing that only intellectual and artistic play in which one drew freely on all one's faculties could restore man's wholeness. In the modern factory, by contrast, play approaches the zero degree, and labor becomes abstract labor in which only labor time has value. As E. P. Thompson explained, money is paid not for a finished product but for time "spent": "Not the task but the value of time when reduced to money is dominant" (359).

William reflects a version of this antinomy when he berates himself while pondering the industrial landscape: "You have chosen trade and you shall be a tradesman! . . . Look at the sooty smoke in that hollow, and know that there is your post! There you cannot dream, you cannot speculate and theorize—there you shall out and work!" (48). William opposes intellectual speculation and theory not to the particular work he performs in the countinghouse but to a general "work" ("you cannot speculate and theorize—there you shall out and work!"). They are the very opposite of work, forms of play denied him in a space ruled by clock time. "Eight o' clock strikes! your hands are thawed, get to work!" William tells himself (72). But this very manual form of mental labor—copying something into one's "hand"—does not simply turn William into another factory laborer. Insofar as his work is derivative, it actually places him behind such workers. He merely facilitates *distribution*, a symbolically secondary component of industrial capitalism, while the laborers engage in *production*. Like Marx, for whom knowledge was either constant capital or stored labor but in either case nonproductive, Brontë depicts intellectual labor, at least under these conditions, as second to physical labor. Literally. Though he "sprang" from bed the minute the "factory bells rang," and though he "hurried down the street," William tells us, he nonetheless finds that "the factory workpeople had preceded [him] by nearly an hour, and the mill was all lighted up and in full operation" (70–71). In a world run strictly by the clock, William finds himself haunted by the fear that he is in some sense "behind time": "I started up imagining that I had overslept myself and should be behind time at the counting-house" (88).

But if it is a foregone conclusion that William will leave this dehumanizing place for one in which he can indulge what he calls his "cherished in secret, Imagination," the terms of his departure are nonetheless surprising (62). William's release from the countinghouse is presented as a rejection of trade that is also not a rejection. He makes it clear that he would be unhappy if he stayed, but he makes it equally clear that he would not have left of his own accord. "I had got away from Bigden Close without any breach of resolution; without any injury to my self-respect," William says after Edward fires him, wrongly believing that William has insulted him among the townspeople; "I had not forced circumstances; circumstances had freed me" (76). A worker who does not cancel a contract on a whim, whose "self-respect" depends on his behaving always "faithfully, punctually, diligently" (55) and on his always exhibiting "punctuality, industry, and accuracy" (63), is as far removed from the leisured aristocrat as can be. He is in fact a model employee. "I hate irregular and slovenly habits," he reports (65). If William implicitly rejects trade, he does not reject the attributes trade requires. If he opposes intellectual speculation and theory to work, it is not for fear of work. He rejects trade, finally, because he fears wasted labor—labor that is less productive because it is simple. By turning translating into copying, the counting-house ignores the highly complex labor of which William's phrenological "bumps" suggest he is capable. "What good can your bumps of ideality, comparison, self-esteem, conscientiousness, do you here?" a friend asks him (60). "Ideality" and "comparison" denote abilities of creativity and evaluation that are not being tapped, and while "self-esteem" and "conscientiousness" might make him a good employee, they cannot be turned to his own profit in the factory. Boiled down to pure labor, mental labor leaves its producer subservient to capital.

III

"It is no strange thing," the journal *The School and the Teacher* claimed at mid-century, "that men who in education, tastes and habits have all the qualifications of 'gentlemen' should regard themselves as worthy of something very much higher than the treatment of a servant and the wages of a mechanic. What in short the teacher desires is that his 'calling' shall rank as a 'profession'; that the name of 'schoolmaster' shall ring as grandly on the ear as that of 'clergyman' or 'solicitor'" (qtd. in Altick 240n4).[8] When William Crimsworth starts anew in Belgium, he begins what will be a long and illustrious career as a schoolmaster. Crimsworth's career as an educator begins in a boys' boarding school, moves to a girls' school, and reaches its apex when he lands a university post while simultaneously opening and operating a school with his wife Frances.

William Crimsworth's meteoric rise through the ranks of this protoprofession is another form of translation: the translation of faces and bodies into terms of inner worth. Throughout the novel, Crimsworth is uniquely able to decipher faces, which he correlates with the pages of a book (46). While William and Edward both, for example, can read French and German business correspondence, Edward cannot read a countenance: "He was trying to read my character," the protagonist says as his brother watches him work, "but I felt as secure against his scrutiny as if I had on a casque with the visor down—or rather I showed him my countenance with the confidence that one would show an unlearned man a letter written in Greek; he might see lines, and trace characters, but he could make nothing of them" (53). The younger Crimsworth owns a weapon his older brother must do without or, rather, to follow William's own self-correction in which he refines the vehicle of his metaphor from that of the costume of a medieval knight ("casque with visor") to that of an internalized language (Greek), he possesses embodied property his brother lacks. Edward's capital equips him to run a mill, while the protagonist's bumps permit him to run the business of learning itself, to oversee the classroom where his labor can now be productive, manufacturing for his students "praise and blame in very small retail parcels" (163).

Unlike reading business correspondence, reading skulls would seem to be an aesthetic practice, a practice in which one discriminates subtle differences rather than distilling objects into their objectified exchange value. But the logic of the factory persists as Brontë rewrites aesthetic play into labor so that it can possess market value. Overseeing translation rather than performing it, William Crimsworth schools his Belgian students in Latin and English, while he himself uses phrenology to translate persons into commensurable values. Consequently, although the romantic space of a girls' school replaces the hard space of the factory, the classroom in which Crimsworth ultimately finds his calling nonetheless looks strikingly like the mill from which he has fled.

At the girls' school, Crimsworth finds an unruly mob, "interrupt[ing him] perpetually with little silly questions and uncalled-for remarks," but by quickly reading their characters and establishing a hierarchy among them, he establishes order (115). "My first business this afternoon," Crimsworth relates, "consisted in reading the list of places for the month." He provides a student ranking, listing not the relative merits and faults of their papers but the details of their heads (referred to in the novel as "organs"), ending at "the bottom of the list" with that pupil whose "organs of benevolence, veneration, conscientiousness, adhesiveness, were singularly small, those of self-esteem, firmness, destructiveness, combativeness, preposterously large" (129). "As much as in the factory interior," Roger Cooter wrote, "the phrenology head was an advertisement for a more automated reality in which character itself reduced to digits on a graph" (112).[9] In the classroom, political economy was reformulated as a pedagogical economy, but rather than being inserted within the division of labor, the professor presided over it. "I felt in myself complete power to manage my pupils," Crimsworth says (117).

In the detailed accounts of lessons and the descriptions of his strict management of students, Crimsworth's classroom takes shape as a Taylorist utopia, a place Brontë described in the same vocabulary she used to describe the mill—a place where "a wasteful expense of energy and labour" (160) must be avoided and all "vacant moments must be turned to profitable account" (92). But even as Crimsworth pursues his "system," rationalizing his educational efforts by reducing his students to the shapes of their skulls, the novel attempts to protect Crimsworth himself from the threat of universal equivalence (97). Crimsworth's mental labor must be seen to be work so that it can be inserted into the market—and thus demand compensation—but it must at the same time be differentiated from manual labor by being depicted as work performed under his own auspices, autonomous rather than supervised labor.

One critical passage demonstrates Crimsworth's professional autonomy. In doing so, it dissolves both the purity of aesthetic autonomy and the purity of the middle-class girl in order to disclose the labor embodied in what at first appear to be effortless productions of nature. In a discussion dedicated to convincing us of Crimsworth's disinterested rather than prurient interest in his female students, allaying "any doubt" the "incredulous reader" might possess as to Crimsworth's "conscientious self-denial and self-control," Crimsworth says that "a master stands in a somewhat different relation towards a pretty light-headed . . . girl to that occupied by a partner at a ball, or a gallant on the promenade" (148). "To the tutor," he continues, "female charms are like tapestry hangings of which the wrong side is continually turned towards him; and even when he sees the smooth, neat, external surface he so well knows what knots, long stitches, and jagged ends are behind that he has scarce temptation to admire too fondly the seemly forms and bright colors exposed to general view" (149). Adorno wrote that "it is impossible to conceive of the autonomy of art without covering up work" and it is just this covering up that *The Professor* prohibits (qtd. in Bürger 35). The underside of the beautiful tapestry betrays the cost of its production: in the long stitches, we see work's long stretches; in the pressure of knots and the hurried jagged ends, we see material necessity. It is this side, the side of labor, that Crimsworth occupies. After all, his objectified labor is embodied in the finished girl his finishing school produces. Paradoxically, then, Crimsworth's exposure of art's labor and, thus, its lack of autonomy enables him to achieve the disinterested interest that characterizes professional autonomy. Restoring labor to aesthetics, the novel pulls intellectual labor into political economy and makes it value-able. But by depicting intellectual labor as artisanal rather than industrial, the passage means to reserve for that labor an autonomy not generally possible under industrial production.[10]

The Professor displaces economic desire onto sexual desire so that Crimsworth can illustrate his autonomy without ever disavowing or, for that matter, even dampening his economic appetites. By presenting Crimsworth as outside the sexual or marriage market within which the "partner at a ball" and the "gallant on the promenade" circulate, the novel signals his professional autonomy without needing to define him against the commercial market it desires for him. This displacement facilitates the novel's critique of the principle of aesthetic autonomy with its implicit conceptual reliance on nature. What appears effortless in the passage—the girl's beauty—has in fact a history of effort behind it. The novel uncovers the hidden intellectual labor—the lessons in elocution, the cultivation of judgment and taste—so that its costs can be tallied, but while such an accounting enhances the value of the girl's instructor, it necessarily subtracts from the girl's. She no longer appears beautiful but rather duplicitous, hiding her rough underbelly from suitors. By exposing the labor of aesthetics, Brontë uncouples aristocratic independence from disinterest, and she also breaks the tie between disinterest and the middle-class angel.[11] Defining her modern professional, Brontë simultaneously disables his two competitors in the market for disinterest.

Brontë's insistence on labor where aesthetics once played makes concealed labor visible. As a result, beauty itself must be reevaluated. Describing one student, Crimsworth says:

> Raven-black hair, very dark eyes, absolutely regular features . . . formed in her that assemblage of points whose union many persons regard as the perfection of beauty. How, with the tintless pallor of her skin and the classic straightness of her lineaments, she was able to look sensual, I don't know. I think her lips and eyes contrived the affair, and the result left no uncertainty on the beholder's mind. She was sensual now, and in ten years' time she would be coarse—promise plain was written in her face of much future folly. (114–15)

Here it is not a past that is unearthed by the professional reader of faces but a future foretold. In either case, time is restored to what might otherwise appear to belong not to history but to timeless nature.

If the novel argues that beauty tries to distract our attention from time, then it makes sense that what first attracts our narrator's attention to Frances, the student who becomes his wife, is her overt submission to time:

> When I first cast my eyes on her, she sat looking fixedly down, her chin resting on her hand, and she did not change her attitude till I commenced the lesson. None of the Belgian girls would have retained one position, and that a reflective one, for the same length of time. (151)

Later in the novel, Crimsworth comments, "I knew she could retain a thinking attitude for a long time without change" (194). Such an ability suggests the self-discipline required by the modern economy, the ability to subordinate oneself to time rather than evade it. The other striking feature about this description of Frances is that we are given very few features at all: "I know well enough that I have left on your mind's eye no distinct picture of her," Crimsworth says, "I have not painted her complexion, nor her eyes, nor her hair, nor even drawn the outline of her shape" (152–53). Crimsworth's withholding of details is not, he tells us, perversity but ignorance: "It is not my intention to communicate to you a knowledge I myself gained little by little" (152). Though he has read every face he encounters instantaneously, providing us with immediate and elaborate analyses, he claims to be incapable of reading this face at a glance. Instead, what we see as the tale continues is Frances at work.

As Crimsworth places Frances on a regimen of reading, translating, and writing (176), the novel's representation of intellectual labor passes from his own work as professor to hers as pupil. The "benefits of [Crimsworth's] system" (176) quickly become apparent:

> Frances did not become pale or feeble in consequence of her sedentary employment; perhaps the stimulus it communicated to her mind counterbalanced the inaction it imposed on her body. She changed, indeed she changed obviously and rapidly; but it was for the better. (175)

Work that does not exercise the body—which, indeed, "impose[s]" "inaction" on the body—has material effects nonetheless: "A clearness of skin almost bloom, and a plumpness almost embonpoint, softened the decided lines of her feature. Her figure . . . became rounder" (175). In Crimsworth's classroom, translation becomes not copying, not derivative imitation, but original production. After practicing translation, Frances begins "composition[s]." "Such occupation," Crimsworth informs us, "seemed the very breath of her nostrils, and soon her improved productions wrung from me the avowal that those qualities in her that I had termed taste and fancy ought rather to have been denominated judgment and imagination" (174). Inspiration—"breath"—is tied to the body—"nostrils"—in a metaphorical formulation, the awkwardness of which might be seen as insisting that even in the realm of "judgment and imagination," mental labor is also material. This sentence is noteworthy, however, primarily for another reason: it undermines labor even as it intends to reinforce it.

What Crimsworth "had termed taste and fancy" are not presented to us as developing into "judgment and imagination" through steady practice but rather as "qualities" that exist in her which he had not yet properly appreciated. Generating a rhetorical effect found throughout Brontë's prose, this sentence portrays Frances's hard work not as producing something but as disclosing something—in this case, inherent aesthetic ability. Brontë works to restore labor to intellectual activity and yet the urgency with which she wishes to render this immaterial labor material leads her to repeatedly present that labor less as work after all and more as a form of property or capital. Similarly, Crimsworth later notices that Frances's "mental power manifested [itself] gradually and steadily" (176). "Mental power" exists a priori; it is just more or less visible. He, to pluck another example from many, does not depict Frances as responding to circumstances in particular ways but rather Frances "display[s]" a faculty when "circumstances . . . forced it out of the depths where it burned latent" (262). Talent, ability, mental power, and capacity exist. They are only more or less visible—on display or latent.

Throughout the novel, the prose depicts activities that occur over time as qualities figured as objects or people. For example, Brontë does not simply show our hero behaving cautiously and tactfully but rather capitalizes "Caution" and "Tact" and refers to them as his "faculties" (63). Immaterial events that happen in time are understood in spatial, quasi-material terms: Crimsworth does not "think" but rather "thoughts occup[y] [his] mind" (90). One particularly dizzying passage describes Crimsworth's love for Frances: she, we learn, is "my best object of sympathy on earth . . . my ideal of the shrine in which to seal my stores of love; personification of discretion and forethought, of diligence and perseverance, of self-denial and self-control—those guardians, those trusty keepers of the gift I longed to confer on her" (195–96). Frances moves from being an object, to an ideal, to a personification, and then is dropped from the prose as all that she personifies—discretion, forethought, diligence, and perseverance—is itself personified in the form of "guardians" and "trusty keepers." The tangible—the person—becomes intangible—a set of qualities—and then the intangible is personified, rendered tangible. Throughout the novel, immaterial qualities take on a solidity of their own, as if the novel needs to distinguish attributes from the person who possesses them so that it may more readily assess their worth.

The rhetorical twists in which, in a sense, "verbs" become "nouns" is symptomatic, a measure of the novel's desire to professionalize intellectual labor. Even Frances, at first exempted from phrenological assessment, gets "read" just like every other character, as the novel attempts to confer upon her the prestige of innate property. Assessing the "calibre of her capacity," Crimsworth finds that the place where intelligence is located is highly developed while the space indicating the animal instincts is underdeveloped: "The shape of her head was different [from the other students']; the superior part more developed; the base considerably less so" (156, 151). The novel replaces aesthetic beauty with something we might call "embodied intelligence," intelligence that is stored within, and at the same time manifested upon, the body. Thus, when we do finally hear Crimsworth call someone (Frances) beautiful, he declares it in the following, strange formulation: "The intelligence of her face seemed beauty to me" (201). Intelligence has become a property of the body ("of her face") and, as such, can now be considered beautiful—just as, conversely, even those conventionally understood to boast "personal attractions" look instead disfigured when the expert's eye notices upon them the "brand of mental inferiority" (149–50).

In the novel's logic, what one does becomes rather what one is capable of doing as indicated by embodied properties. Crimsworth's student ranking, for example, does not evaluate what each student has learned or failed to learn but rather what each student is capable of learning, her "aptitude for cultivation," to borrow a phrase from Brontë's letters about her own students (Wise 1: 199). Once transformed into innate property or capital, ability can then act as a prophylactic against proletarianization. The language of "aptitude," "faculties," or "organs" converts into an asset what would, as mental labor, be leeched into abstract time. Intellectual assets not only ostensibly protect intellectual labor from reduction to manual labor, they also render their owner superior to the industrial capitalist. "I kept the padlock of silence," Crimsworth tells us about his conduct at the mill, "on mental wealth of which [Edward] was no sharer" (63). Crimsworth's "mental wealth" is superior, the novel wants us to believe, to his brother's more conventional kind, because whereas a capitalist can lose his money capital though bad business or bad luck, the professional cannot in the same sense lose mental capital: it is inseparable from its owner. While it can be abstracted from the professional (as ability, aptitude, or IQ, for instance), it cannot be separated from him. Learning at one point that Edward has lost everything, we are to understand William's steady rise as intrinsic to his particular vocation, one that draws on a form of capital immune to the risks endemic to economic capital.

One might argue that this tendency to turn activities into measurable abilities and measurable abilities, in turn, into "wealth" simply reproduces at the sentence level the book's larger plan wherein the labor of Crimsworth and Frances eventually earns them what Brontë calls in her preface "a small competency" but what is in the book enough capital for them to retire in comfort and ensure that their son receives an elite education. Brontë, then, simply lays bare the modus operandi of the professional who, to recall Perkin's words, "transform[s] a service into an income-yielding property" (7). Somehow, though, the effect here is not one of mutual reinforcement but of contradiction. The nominalizing tendency of Brontë's prose in general, and of the language of phrenology in particular, radically undercuts the novel's emphasis on the merit of labor. By showcasing the phrenological work of reading character, Brontë ironically privileges a form of intellectual labor that purports to determine the value of someone without needing to evaluate her labor.[12] The professor's students, for example, do not need to put pen to paper for him to know their worth: "In less than five minutes," Crimsworth says after scanning the girls' heads on the very first day of class, "[the students] had revealed to me their characters" (115). Representing work in the form of natural property (bumps, organs, faculties, gifts, and the like) visible to the expert's eye, Brontë does the very thing she forbids of beauty in particular and aesthetics in general: she erases the time of labor. The mental labor she is at pains to depict disappears into mental properties that look like nothing more than the apparently effortless productions of nature.

Like the later IQ test, phrenology assumed that people differed from each other in their innate abilities, that these innate abilities were open to assessment by educational professionals, and that professional evaluations would then dictate the proper—or, more to the point, natural—stations for individuals in society. In place of class struggle, the professional claimed to substitute a hierarchy with a meritocracy structured around "the vertical career hierarchy rather than the horizontal connection of class" (Perkin, *Rise* 9) that was putatively the by-product not of power or money but of an unmediated nature. "The meritocratic illusion," Daniel Cottom writes, "is the belief that one can isolate merit within a society by means of a neutral rationality and thus promote a society that stratifies itself according to the laws of nature" (16). The language that developed to underwrite the expert class, a language of "natural talents" and "intellectual gifts," echoed Kant in his use of nature to underwrite art. In both cases, nature confers authority and prestige by obscuring material history.

The problem with *The Professor*, then, is not, as Neville Newman would have it, that intellectual labor is not real labor. Citing Brontë's claim in her preface that "whatever small competency [her hero] might gain should be won by the sweat of his brow," Newman says, "The sweat he expends [at a girls' boarding school] is metaphorical at best" (11). *The Professor* pointedly refuses the assumption that immaterial labor does not count as real work, that metaphorical sweat cannot convey true effort. The problem is rather that an unresolved tension runs through the novel. As I've argued throughout, bringing intellect to the market in the first half of the nineteenth century required representing it in terms of productive work rather than leisured play, while ensuring that mental labor did not get reduced on that market to manual labor seemed to require that it be represented in terms of innate capital. Both forms of representation enabled Brontë to illuminate what was previously invisible—the one by uncovering hidden labor, the other by materializing the immaterial—but the latter representation (innate capital) effectively undoes the time necessary for the former (labor). Reifying intellectual capacity as timeless, natural property that is simply more or less visible, Brontë ironically ends up reinforcing a simplistic definition of labor. Labor becomes, finally, simply pure labor—empty time that does not produce anything although it might disclose something. In short, Brontë markets her professional by providing two definitions, one of which threatens to cancel the other.

Crimsworth's "mental wealth" (63) becomes actual wealth as he and his wife accrue "capital to invest" (280) and "realize an independency" (280). The expectations Brontë raised in the preface do, then, make the ending of the novel come as something of a surprise. That the "small competency" has accumulated from teaching rather than physical labor is not surprising but that it is not teaching alone that earns Crimsworth his independence is unexpected. It is earned rather by an uneasy combination of teaching and investing. In one brief paragraph, we learn that the idyllic pastoral life to which the Crimsworths retire owes itself as much to economic capital as to mental capital and labor:

> Behold us now at the close of the ten years, and we have realized an independency. The rapidity with which we attained this end had its origin in three reasons:—Firstly, we worked so hard for it; secondly, we had no incumbrances to delay success; thirdly, as soon as we had capital to invest, two well-skilled counselors, one in Belgium, one in England . . . gave us a word each of advice as to the sort of investment to be chosen. The suggestion made was judicious, and being promptly acted on, the result proved gainful; I communicated details to [the counselors]; nobody else can be interested in hearing them. (280)

The risky market in which Edward places William's capital appears to be secure enough when mediated by experts ("well-skilled counselors") whose "judicious" tips are followed by a professional who appreciates the value of time and "promptly act[s]." Representing investment in the market as if William were still somehow talking about professional labor does not allow Brontë to get through the passage smoothly, however. Instead, she has

Crimsworth blame the reader for the fact that she herself preferred not to elaborate: "nobody else can be interested." Still she chose this recipe for independence, as if at the last moment she wished to write away the dilemma that disfigured her text, as if representing labor combining with capital as unremarkable would make readers less likely to remark on the uneasy combination of mental labor and mental capital that constitutes her own professional.

IV

"Because political economy and aesthetics were once part of the same discourse," Mary Poovey writes, "and because their separation was never complete, each discourse continued to haunt the other in the form of vestigial traces" ("Aesthetics" 82). If in many nineteenth-century texts the terms of political economy and aesthetics "haunt" each other, then in *The Professor* the latter is collapsed into the former as the practices of aesthetics are written into market language and social, extra-economic relations depicted in economic terms. Marx argued that feudal relations were social relations first and economic relations second while capitalism reversed that priority so that the laborer mistakenly imagines himself to be voluntarily exchanging his labor-power. In Brontë's novel, however, it is as if everything involving William, particularly social relations, has been filtered through the logic of market equivalence so the reader might understand his every judgment to be perfectly free and autonomous, made under no emotional obligation or affective influence, no compromise of his professional independence. To take one example, interactions among family members are described as "transaction[s]" in which "mental power" possesses the capacity to "extort" others (176). When a friend offers to help him, to take another example, Crimsworth replies with no hint of irony or whimsy, "I am in your debt already; you did me an important service when I was at X . . . that service I have never repaid, and at present I decline positively adding another item to the account" (227–28). It seems that services, even between friends, require payment if one is not to be compromised. Crimsworth's eccentricity has a logic that makes sense only when the professional is under particular duress to establish the value of his services. In order to avoid any appearance of impropriety, in order to appear perfectly impartial, the professional must refuse any gifts—those items that are offered as if outside the logic of exchange but which might demand, nonetheless, a return. Far from being procured, then, by distance or removal from the market, Crimsworth's professional independence is achieved only through the most thoroughgoing adoption of market logic.[13]

In the example above, Crimsworth is careful to refuse what might be perceived as "the interests in disinterestedness," to borrow Martha Woodmansee's phrase (11). Embracing market discourse ironically protects him from any self-interested motives that might accompany allegedly disinterested aid. Crimsworth's suspicion of disinterest is not unlike the implicit suspicion evinced in critical arguments that illustrate how the professional or the artist rhetorically enacts his distance from the market. In such arguments, distance from the market becomes a kind of credit that then ensures the value of the professional or artist. Woodmansee's important *The Author, Art, and the Market*, for example, argues that the "momentous shift from an instrumentalist theory of art to the modern theory of art as an autonomous object that is to be contemplated disinterestedly" was a reaction to a fast-growing bourgeois market for literature (32). As certain poets and writers found themselves neglected by this new public, they developed a theory that could rescue aesthetic value from market determination. (See chapter 4 for a more extensive discussion of Woodmansee's book.) The articulation of aesthetic disinterest was itself, then, far from disinterested. Woodmansee's analysis is persuasive and, as a kind of elaboration upon Raymond Williams's observation that aesthetic ideology contained "elements of compensation," it is extremely useful (36). However, it neglects the other side of aesthetic ideology, a side Williams was quick to acknowledge: its expression of, as he wrote, "certain human values, capacities, energies, which the development towards an industrial civilization was felt to be threatening or even destroying" (36). And yet, though right to acknowledge the progressive side of aesthetic ideology, Williams slightly misstates the case. It is not that aesthetics preserved older values but rather that aesthetics, born in the same moment as, and in opposition to, political economy, offers an alternative system of value. With aesthetics, Peter Bürger writes, "a new way of perceiving that is immune to the means-ends rationality comes into existence" (41). That aesthetics produced this new mode by repressing labor indicates that its alternative system is one side of a coin whose other side is political economy.

Once its professional's economic interests are secured, *The Professor* does finally return to the issue of aesthetic disinterest. In a scene that might be considered the late counterpart to that early scene in which a friend teases Crimsworth, "Carry your intellect and refinement to the market and tell me in a private note what price is bid for them," the same friend (Hunsden) asks Frances about the value of "poetical associations":

> "Mademoiselle, what is an association? I never saw one. What is its length, breadth, weight, value—aye, value? What price will it bring in the market?"

> "Your portrait, to anyone who loved you, would, for the sake of association, be without price."
>
> That inscrutable Hunsden heard this remark and felt it rather acutely, too, somewhere; for he coloured—a thing not unusual for him, when hit unawares on a tender point. (261)

Art's refusal of exchange value ("without price") is recovered here, but it is, significantly, by way of Frances not Crimsworth, who places himself clearly outside the discussion, not participating in it but calmly commenting upon it. Frances, it is true, has by this point in the novel become a kind of proxy for Crimsworth. Or, perhaps more accurately, Frances picks up where Crimsworth leaves off as the novel transfers its energy from the one to the other. It is Frances whom we follow in the novel's final chapter as she moves through her school, displaying her "superior mind" for her students' benefit (274). Having given the professional proximity to the market, it is as if Brontë then wished to give him distance, and realized that the fulfillment of that wish required beginning a new story with a protagonist who has not so thoroughly internalized market logic.

If the novel is a failure, as so many critics and readers have charged, then it is not because Brontë was unable effectively to use a male narrator.[14] Nor is it because Brontë's "proper gifts were consciously denied full play in [the novel]," as one critic notes, relying on both the language of intellectual property Brontë helped popularize as well as the aesthetic vocabulary of "play" she tried to pull from circulation (Ward 102). *The Professor* fails because the novel's apparent success at producing a marketable professional leaves its readers and even perhaps itself deeply dissatisfied, desiring a story quite different from the one that just unfolded. It is not only that the capital-and-labor theory of value underwriting her prosperous professional is conflicted at best and self-imploding at worst, but that the novel produces a professional so market-oriented that it seems, by negation, to trigger a longing for another professional, one more disposed to subordinate the market to higher concerns, one for whom service is not first and foremost transformable into an income-yielding property but is rather service for others without regard for self. At its most effective, the professional class convinces us that it is "a class which is necessarily not-for-itself" but for others (Frow 127). This rhetoric of service is, of course, self-serving insofar as it furnishes the professional class with moral authority, cultural prestige, and material income, but it is also an ideal worth preserving, particularly in an era of widespread deprofessionalization. It is an ideal that insists that market logic is not the only logic, an insistence first expressed in the notion of aesthetic disinterest and one that, as Herbert Marcuse once wrote, "keeps alive the best desires of men amidst a bad reality" (102).

I do not want to conclude this chapter, however, by flourishing the ideal of disinterestedness. To do so would be to freeze the dialectic between the regressive and progressive sides of aesthetic ideology, merely championing one side over the other. Today, as humanities professors are increasingly called upon to justify what we do in market terms, we are especially likely to find Brontë's market-oriented protagonist repugnant. But a better response than repugnance with its accompanying retreat to the progressive side of the aesthetic ideal is to ask whether this narrative of professorial professionalization offers any clues to our crisis of professorial deprofessionalization, a crisis best documented by colleges and universities' growing reliance on adjunct labor. *The Professor* suggests that professional labor challenged aesthetics in order to insert itself into the market but that it did so at an enormous cost—the cost of condemning itself to a never-ending struggle to distinguish itself from virtually every other form of labor under capital. The novel distinguishes professional labor by depicting mental labor as a form of capital—mental capital—which authorizes the professional's status as manager rather than managed. In this way, though, the novel implicates itself in what Adorno called the "age-old culpability that lies in the divorce of physical from mental labour" (323), erroneously imagining that such a divorce protects mental labor from proletarianization. But mental labor is never immune to the danger of being modeled upon routinized physical labor and, thus, subordinated to capital. This is what Crimsworth finds when he works for his brother and what scores of humanities PhDs find today when they look for tenure-track jobs only to find a system increasingly designed to pay them by the course. *The Professor* prompts us to ask: Is there a way to fight for intellectual autonomy that foregrounds rather than represses mental labor's similarities to other forms of labor?

CHAPTER TWO

Becoming Professional:
Time in David Copperfield

I. A MOST UNBECOMING PROFESSIONAL: DAVEY COPPERFIELD

D. A. Miller's "Secret Subjects, Open Secrets" and Mary Poovey's "The Man-of-Letters Hero: *David Copperfield* and the Professional Writer" have proven so persuasive that George Levine recently admitted that he cannot "think about *David Copperfield* again without a certain embarrassment at what seems now almost blatant celebration of self-discipline and self-sacrifice in the interest of bourgeois identity and bourgeois ideology" (*Dying to Know* 6).[1] For both Miller and Poovey, David falls woefully short of his own self-perception. In Miller, this lack of self-knowledge makes him no different from any of the novel's characters, all of whom are liberal subjects trapped by a putative opposition between freedom and incarceration. In Poovey, as my introductory chapter discussed, David's status as a professional makes him especially culpable and his self-ignorance shields him from knowledge of his professional hypocrisy. In this chapter, I offer a new interpretation of Victorian studies' most unbecoming professional, but since I do not address Miller or Poovey's arguments directly in my reading, I first wish to mention two scholars that do. In their own readings of the same novel, Rachel Ablow and Matthew Titolo clear the space for arguments like my own.

Ablow and Titolo incorporate Foucauldian arguments, but they mark their distance from earlier readings by transforming what appeared in those readings as "the inescapable pathos of [liberalism's] double bind" into the "properly dialectical exercise of its positive and negative aspects," to borrow some phrases from Fredric Jameson ("Theoretical Hesitation" 284). Ablow and Titolo assume two things. First, they assume that the novelist was aware of the ideologies at work in his text. Thus, Dickens is Foucault's peer rather than his archive: "The typical Dickens novel," Titolo writes, "grapples with the same power asymmetries analyzed in the typical Michel Foucault essay" (186). Ablow writes, "by contrast with those who have claimed to reveal [*David Copperfield's*] previously-concealed interpellative effects, I argue that the novel not only calls attention to its disciplinary agenda, it defines it as the principal source of its literary and ethical value" (24).[2] Second, in the work of Titolo and Ablow, as well as others writing recently, the ideologies themselves are not as totalizing as previously assumed. Whereas Poovey understood the professional to be thoroughly duplicitous and Miller described liberal subjects as irrevocably "boxed in," critics who follow the logics of Ablow and Titolo are more likely to view the professional as an ambivalent figure and to view autonomy as relative and partial rather than always, already impossible.

Ablow's argument rests on reading *Copperfield's* Agnes as Dickens's endorsement of the ideal for ideal's sake. Feminist critics complain that the domestic ideal imposed an unreal standard of self-renunciation and that, by circulating this ideal in fiction, novelists encouraged real women to sacrifice themselves at the altar of the household gods. Ablow exempts Dickens from this charge by claiming that Agnes "is never posited as a model for a person" but is "a kind of fiction that can serve as the object of one's affections without claiming any empirical accuracy" (33). David requires a series of ideals—Steerforth, Dora, Agnes—around which to organize his ambition and motivate himself, and Agnes is the final ideal whose unreality makes her no less important and useful to David's progress.

Ablow's essay, in short, argues for the productive power of the ideal. The suspicious model demystifies the ideal without acknowledging its power to motivate behavior whereas Ablow's thesis spotlights precisely that power of motivation. Poovey demonstrates that the housewife's "love" is in fact domestic labor that has been rendered invisible by the public/private divide. Ablow, on the other hand, does not strive to demystify "love" but rather to show that "*David Copperfield* seeks to encourage love in its readers" by illustrating how the idealization of the love object prompts the protagonist to better himself and the reader's love for the novel, in turn, "prompts the reader to better herself" (24). Positioning itself against "disciplinary" arguments that expose idealism's hypocrisy, Ablow's argument acknowledges what Marcuse, speaking specifically of the principle of aesthetic disinterest, called "the critical force of the ideal," which "keeps alive the best desires of men amidst a bad reality" (102–3). Ablow, it seems, wishes to hold on to the possibility that one's labor—professional or domestic—might sometimes be performed for the sake of others rather than for oneself (or, more accurately, *experienced* as performed for others even as it is also undertaken for oneself).

While Ablow expresses a dialectical impulse in her insistence on the ideal's positive and productive dimension, Titolo is more self-consciously dialectical, careful to show how positive and negative functions inhere within the same ideal. Like Ablow, Titolo focuses on the same set of issues that interest Poovey: professionalism and its negotiation of public/private dualism. On the one hand, to Poovey, the private sphere of the domestic angel, the hearth where labor ostensibly is not labor because it is love, offers professionalism an established ideological resource upon which to draw in order to sanitize itself. To Titolo, on the other hand, private/public do not have the discreteness Poovey's argument takes for granted. "We should view Dickens," he writes, "as deeply unsettled about the normative boundaries between public and private that we generally assume his novels endorse. For Dickens, public and private are not mutually exclusive but rather mutually implicated; each provides the space in which the true meaning of the other can be elaborated" (174–75). If, as Titolo says later, professionalism *does* draw ideologically on the idyllic space of the home, this is not simple mystification. He writes:

> Dickens both fears and values individual and collective enterprises that claimed exemption from the economic reason which he saw as a particularly modern scourge. And Dickens often parodies his own idealizations; he knows, for example, that the household/office, even if protected from the worst excesses of the industrial marketplace by a guild ideology, might be another ruse of economic reason. So although Dickens tends to idealize David's various displaced families, his impulse is to call people to account just at the moment when a noncontractual language of emotion would seem more suited to his pastoral argument. (180–81)

Titolo goes on to show that David himself "realizes that his idealized, patriarchal guild masks its own calculating logic" (181). He takes pains, in fact, to show us how David (and, thus, Dickens) is cognizant of the ideological underpinnings of professionalism, *not* disingenuous about them. If, in Poovey's reading, David is "self-serving" (118), "manipulat[ive]" (117), and "complicitous" (120), then, in Titolo's, he "threaten[s] to expose" (173), "demystify[ies]" (177), "realizes" (181), and "self-conscious[ly] debunk[s]" (181).

Dialectical thinking entails grasping the positive and the negative at once: "Marx powerfully urges us to do the impossible," writes Jameson, "namely, to think . . . positively *and* negatively all at once: to achieve, in other words, a type of thinking that would be capable of grasping the demonstrably baleful features of capitalism along with its extraordinary and liberating dynamism simultaneously within a single thought and without attenuating any of the force of either judgment" (*Postmodernism* xi). Absolving Dickens, David, and the novel of ideological subterfuge by demonstrating that these entities were as suspicious of liberal ideology as we are ourselves, Titolo frees us up to grasp dialectically those "remainders" that find representation in the Victorian novel, those residual, non-instrumentalized pockets that persist within the modern discourse of professionalism.

In Titolo's argument, noncommodified elements survive in professional practices despite modernity's iron cage, because the professional office takes the shape of the "enchanted enclave" of the precapitalist guild. Harkening back to an archaic model, the professional resists being ruled solely by means-ends rationality. "For Dickens, as for many nineteenth-century writers, morally sound authority requires that patron-client bonds survive as ideological husks of an older, enchanted relationship," he writes (179). In what follows, I also offer a post-Foucauldian reading of *David Copperfield*, but whereas Titolo finds that only the preindustrial past offers rhetorical resources for withstanding Victorian capitalism's cash nexus, I argue that it is ironically the most rationalized aspect of the Victorian present—factory labor—that provides this novel with the material for "disinterest." In my view, David's internalization of the time-discipline the factory clock exemplifies reassures readers that professional autonomy is not an empty ideal behind which lies professional indolence. Since the professional must possess mental capital but cannot speculate on that capital, David is barred from conscious knowledge of what he possesses—the slow, painful movement from unconscious to conscious self-knowledge takes place as his internalization of time-discipline or the requirement that he work in "real" not future-oriented time. Finally, I suggest that the novel's ideal of professionalism is intended to scare up a market for professional services but that acknowledging this does not prevent us from also recognizing that the code of behavior constructed by the novel, and presumably internalized by some of its readers, justifies that market. If we think of the "truth" of *David Copperfield* as its discovery of a formula for cultural capital—a formula that, as I will show, combines the merit of time-disciplined labor with the prestige of innate talent—we might say, with Bourdieu, that "the discovery that someone who has discovered the truth had an interest in doing so in no way diminishes his discovery" (*Pascalian Meditations* 3).

II. Mental Capital and Industrial Time in *David Copperfield*

Though she apparently never wears it, David Copperfield's first wife Dora possesses a watch. Or did possess one. We learn about the watch only when we are told that the couple's servant has absconded with it. The boy "stole Dora's watch," David tells us, "which, like everything else belonging to us, had no particular place of its own; and, converting it into money, spent the produce (he always was a weak-minded boy!) in incessantly riding up and down between London and Uxbridge outside the coach" (657–58). Dora loses track of time (the watch has "no particular place"), thereby unleashing a series of events demonstrating the equivalence of time and money: converting Dora's lost time into money, the boy then loses time himself. A "weak-minded boy"—without someone like David's "resources of intellect" (328), to borrow a phrase from elsewhere in the novel—he lacks both discipline, spending the "produce" immediately, and the power of invention, imagining no more profitable pastime than circling aimlessly. "Moments" are "the elements of profit" in *David Copperfield*, and misappropriated moments represent the potential loss of profit (Marx, *Capital* 1: 233). The Copperfields forfeit their property, while the boy, like the watch's hand traveling equidistant spaces between numerals, covers the same plot of land over and over. Attempting to get ahead by stealing rather than putting in time, he goes nowhere, stuck in empty moments obviously unoccupied by production but not clearly filled by consumption either (eschewing luxury, the frugal boy sits outside the coach).

The problem is not that the watch—the emblem of industrial capitalism and the new time-discipline of the factory, as E. P. Thompson has argued—structures time unnaturally. Rather, the boy's attempt to reach ends ("produce") without means (work) is itself an insult to measurable time. If one expects to get anywhere, Dickens remonstrates, one must submit to time and obey its rules. One must follow the example David has set only a few sentences earlier. Immediately before his discussion of this "unfortunate page," David mentions his own, much more promising career: "I laboured hard at my book, without allowing it to interfere with the punctual discharge of my newspaper duties" (656). The latter clause appears almost as an afterthought—the emphasis ostensibly on the book not the newspaper duties—but it is in fact central to our understanding of the writer David has become. Unlike Dora, David never loses track of time, never falls behind on his newspaper deadlines. Unlike the boy, David respects time; the use of the article "the" rather than the more likely possessive pronoun "my" ("the punctual discharge" as opposed to "my punctual discharge") bespeaks time's objective status and importance to David. Far from espousing the personal, spontaneous writing the Romantics privileged, David's writing proceeds, we might say, like clockwork.[3] Like the factory hand monitoring a machine, David's "hand" appears exchangeable, the style or quality of his particular writing/labor less important than its productive repetition. Yet crucially, if somewhat paradoxically, the first clause of the sentence indicates that David is more than a factory hand: just as we need to hear that the thieving servant possesses a weak mind in addition to (or as the cause of) an inability to manage time, we must hear that David works hard at his own book, his work of imagination, even while discharging his more perfunctory newspaper duties. That is, we must see the power of invention sitting smack up against a mechanical submission to abstract rather than subjective time—mental capital meets industrial labor.

"Each distinctive mode of production or social formation will embody a distinctive bundle of time and space practices and concepts," David Harvey wrote in *The Condition of Postmodernity* (204). Like *Dombey and Son, David Copperfield* is obsessed with time, representing a number of time practices in order, finally, to fix on the one most appropriate to the mid-nineteenth century's emergent professional.[4] Critics commenting on Dickens's fascination with time have tended to do so within generic or psychologizing terms (focusing on his novels as *bildungsromans* or on the status of individual memory), overlooking the larger premise in his novels regarding what might be called, borrowing from Fredric Jameson, "the new rhythms of measurable time" (*Political Unconscious* 152). Such a fundamental project eludes twentieth-century critics for two reasons: 1) The new mode of time—a mode conveniently if reductively grasped in the ubiquitous phrase "time is money"—has become the medium of modern life, something assumed and not analyzed; and 2) at its center, Dickens criticism has placed the author's childhood experience in the blacking warehouse factory and has limited, thereby, the shape of inquiries into Dickens's fictional representations of industrial capitalism. The very last thing we are now prepared to find in a Dickens novel is an endorsement of some aspect of the factory model. Yet that is exactly what we do find. In its attempt to fashion a writing professional, *David Copperfield* presents us with a surprisingly un-Dickensian argument for the temporality of industrial capitalism, differentiating that temporality from other possible modes. The novel refuses in particular, I argue, the temporality of a booming speculative economy—a time contingent on the predictability of a radically unpredictable future or, in Jameson's formulation, "time [as] a new relationship to the future as a space of necessary expectation of revenue and capital accumulation" (*Cultural Turn* 185)—but it also rejects the subjective time of residual Romantic and piecework economies. In short, despite Dickens's well-known objections to factory *life*, *David Copperfield* articulates factory *time*—the organization of labor with regard not to the "ends" but to the regular and predictable use of "objective" time—as the appropriate tempo for the new breed of professional who must not anticipate "ends" (payment for services rendered, professional acclaim, or social success) but rather devote himself to the task at hand.

In an essay on the expanding role played by the "knowledge-producing occupations" in the West, John Frow complains that most accounts of this expansion "offer no theory of the historical change in the composition of capital, and indeed of how it might be possible to understand knowledge as a *form* of capital." "The starting point for such a theory," he suggests, "might be an understanding that knowledge is a moment of both capital and labour, and can be translated into each of these categories" (95). Seeking to resolve or neutralize the apparent contradictions of the new professional by strategically moving between the culturally available vocabularies of finance capital and industrial labor, *David Copperfield* wants to provide us with just such an understanding. Dickens wanted readers to imagine a writing professional whose intelligence resembles capital but whose work habits reproduce the measurable rhythms of labor. In making this argument, I follow Stuart Sherman, whose study of eighteenth-century prose "entails a shift of focus up the social scale," retraining our gaze from "[E. P.] Thompson's laborers [and] Foucault's prisoners" to those for whom time-discipline does not enslave them to others but paradoxically authorizes their autonomy (21).

Examination Nation

In an oft-quoted passage from the novel, the adult David reflects on his childhood stint in a factory:

> It is a matter of some surprise to me, even now, that I can have been so easily thrown away at such an age. A child of excellent abilities, and with strong powers of observation, quick, eager, delicate, and soon hurt bodily and mentally, it seems wonderful to me that nobody should have made any sign on my behalf. But none was made; and I became, at ten years old, a little labouring hind in the service of Murdstone and Grinby. (146)

No critic has pointed out that this is the first passage to explicitly comment on David's "abilities." Before this moment, the adult David, our narrator, has provided very little self-assessment of this objective, empirical type ("excellent abilities, strong powers of observation"), though numerous occasions to do so have presented themselves. When David repeatedly fails at his lessons in the presence of the Murdstones (his very mother begging, "don't be stupid" [51]), for example, we might have been told by the adult David that his childhood self in fact possessed superior faculties. Though he does mention that he had been "apt enough to learn" (50) before the Murdstones, and while he clearly blames their harsh teaching style rather than any personal inadequacy, it is nonetheless striking that only when his childhood self is on the brink of becoming a manual laborer is the adult David compelled to list his qualifications for *mental* labor.

"Every kind of work includes 'mental activity,'" Nicos Poulantzas wrote, "but not every kind of work is located on the mental labour side in the politico-ideological division between mental and manual labour" (237). Beginning with Marx, critics have long argued that the early nineteenth century drains the mind from certain kinds of work and embeds it solely in other forms.[5] More recently, scholars, such as historian of science Simon Schaffer, have demonstrated that the political economy of the 1830s relocates intelligence from the person who manually constructs an object, making it up as he goes, to a mental professional who designs it. In Charles Babbage's scenario, for example, there is a person who does the "real" work, the work of knowledge and invention, and the person who merely physically executes the product of that work. But if we know that the opposition between mental and manual labor was firmly established by the mid-nineteenth century, we know less about the "meritocratic" structure that followed on its heels, the structure by which individuals were allotted to one or the other side of the opposition. During the period in which Dickens wrote *David Copperfield*, the question of education's role in evaluating individuals' mental versus manual qualifications occupied a central space in public debate. (Of course, in the new educational system, one did not qualify for manual labor so much as disqualify for mental labor.) Far more than any other, the instrument by which this new system of qualification both conducted and justified itself was the examination.[6] According to historian John Roach, "the examining method was making converts very rapidly in the late [eighteen] forties" (56).

To Roach, the idea of using examinations to qualify (or, as the case may be, disqualify) candidates for professions stemmed from the prestige of the honors examinations of Oxbridge. Yet, as he also pointed out, the status of the Cambridge Tripos and the Oxford Schools was well-established by 1825. Why, then, he asks, "should it have taken another quarter of a century for the idea of competition and assessment to spread from the universities into public life generally?" (15) The idea awaited, Roach concluded, a shift in the "cultural ethos," a shift "towards free market and open competition of goods and, then, by association, minds":

> The triumph of free competition in all these fields [business, government

> service, and education] took place between 1850 and 1870. In education and administration it started more slowly than in commerce and manufacture, but once the changes gathered impetus, they bit so deeply into the intellectual and cultural structure that their hold has never been shaken. (17)[7]

Even in 1850, one man, John Keble, could complain that "a notion of examinations and talents are everything," alongside "another notion . . . that natural preferences for home and kindred are not to be allowed." "I think," Keble continued, "it is indicative of a certain hard priggishness which is getting to be characteristic of this generation" (qtd. in Roach 21–22). Keble appealed in a sense to biology to argue that "preferences for home and kindred" are "natural"; one naturally prefers blood relations to the strangers thrown up by the modern system of "examinations and talents."

That Dickens placed himself on the reforming side against the likes of Keble should come as no surprise. In the novel at hand, for example, Dickens reverses Keble's accusation that an emphasis on "examinations and talents" indicates "priggishness" by placing the preference for "blood" over brains into the mouths of what is certainly a "priggish" party of petty officials and their wives (ironically, the very class standing to gain the most from the new system). Soliciting a general murmur of approval, the most affected woman at a dinner party exclaims:

> "There are some low minds (not many, I am happy to believe, but there are *some*) that would prefer to do what *I* should call bow down before idols. Positively idols! Before services, intellect, and so on. But these are intangible points. Blood is not so. We see Blood in a nose, and we know it. We meet with it in a chin, and we say, 'There it is! That's blood!' It is an actual matter of fact. We point it out. It admits no doubt." (354)

Dickens's humor resides here in the woman's shortsighted confusion of surface and depth. She impugns "services" and "intellect" for being idols, images without substance, even while she understands "blood" in one-dimensional terms. "Blood" is worthy here for little other reason than that it is visible, confirmed ("matter of fact') in the image of the body, while the worth of services and intellect are repudiated precisely because they have no apparent surface. "Intangible," they admit doubt, eluding one's grasp. It is precisely this desire for immediate confirmation/gratification that the novel will disallow, preferring means instead of ends; and it is exactly this problem of the public's inability to conceptualize the professional—the figure who combines services and intellect—that the novel intends to solve.

"The triumph of the examination system is a major historical landmark," wrote W. J. Reader (116), firmly anchored in the mid-nineteenth century. As the setting of *David Copperfield* is the novelist's present of 1850, the adult narrator describes a childhood presumably of the 1820s or early 1830s, a period before the institution of regular and nationwide school examinations. Indeed, little academic competition of any kind existed at that time. This did not stop Dickens, however, from placing the ethos of "competitive examination" and of "intellect" characterizing his own present at the center of David's education.[8] When David arrives at his first school, the disreputable Salem House, Dickens promptly substitutes "intellect" for "blood" by replacing the signs worn on the body ("we see blood in a nose," the dinner-party lady says) for the gradual revelation of intellectual superiority. Having bitten Mr. Murdstone before he left for school, David is forced by the head of Salem House (Mr. Creakle, a man "who knew nothing himself, but the art of slashing" [82]) to wear a sign on his back that reads, "Take care of him. He bites" (74). If depicted as someone who draws blood rather than embodies it, David's situation nonetheless dramatizes the visual economy of physical power endorsed by the type of school in which patronage trumps merit. The boy marked out for distinction and awarded privileges, is not, as he will be later at Dr. Strong's school, the smartest boy but the boy with old wealth (Steerforth). Yet despite this, David gradually distinguishes himself as "an exception to [the ignorance of] the general body" (90) of students, replacing the visual economy with a latent economy of mental power—if not in the school itself, at least in the minds of the novel's readers.

Dr. Strong's school, on the other hand, is a "school as different from Mr. Creakle's as good is from evil" (225) and thus conducts itself upon "a sound system" (225) of open examination rather than covert patronage. In contrast to David's first day at Salem House on which he is made to wear a kind of false advertisement, his first day at Dr. Strong's consists of an examination designed to honestly access and assess his interior. Although David's knowledge "had so slipped away . . . that now, when [he] is examined," he is "put in the lowest form of the school" (217), he soon begins a meteoric rise through the ranks:

> I am not the last boy in the school [anymore]. I have risen, in a few months, over several heads. But the first boy seems to me a mighty creature, dwelling afar off, whose giddy height is unattainable . . . I chiefly wonder what he'll be when he leaves Dr. Strong's. (252)

The position of "first boy" provides what one Victorian called the "spur of emulation" (qtd. in Roach 4) crucial to the open competition that would produce a generation of capable professionals for England. Here, the awe the "first boy" inspires leads inevitably to daydreams about "what he'll be," what profession he will choose. David rapidly follows in this preprofessional's footsteps. After he has "grow[n] great at Latin verses" (253), has been "refer[red] to . . . in public as a promising scholar" (253), and has "brought new honours home from school" (350), David declares, "I am the head boy, now!" (254).

Intelligence as Capital

Perhaps the greatest proponent of the new system of "examinations and talents" was T. B. Macaulay. Macaulay began arguing for civil service examinations as early as 1833, though it is only in the 1840s that he began selling parliament on the concept. In making his case, Macaulay repeatedly distinguished between "ability" and "mere learning," emphasizing that the object of the test should be to assess the candidate's quality of mind rather than to measure the quantity of his "cramming." According to historian Keith Hope, Macaulay was the first to argue that it is possible to identify a person's "general intelligence," his or her innate mental capacity (qtd. in Hope 9). The examination, Macaulay declared, can abstract from the person his mental caliber regardless of the task and can, thereby, predict the person's future success (or failure) in a profession. As Adrian Wooldridge explains, "Macaulay felt that examinations could accurately predict 'what men will prove to be in life,' since the qualities required for professional success were precisely those tested in the examination room" (167). Like the discourse of speculation finding numerous converts at the same moment—"what distinguished the speculative frenzy of the middle and late forties from all that had gone before, apart from its sheer intensity," writes Richard Altick, "was the number of people involved" ("Speculation and Bankruptcy" 647)—the examination's disclosure of mental capital makes a promise on the future, attempting to disclose history in advance of itself.

I will return to time's relationship to mental and finance capital below, but here what I want to note about Macaulay's distinction—one enthusiastically echoed by others like Sir Charles Trevelyan, Sir Stafford Northcote, and William E. Gladstone—is the line it draws between the laborious acquisition of knowledge (most often symbolized by "cramming" but also called simply "learning") and a quantifiable intelligence.[9] Intelligence is a latent but measurable property, not an activity. Not called upon to demonstrate itself through any sustained effort, it can be abstracted from mental performance on a range of subjects. Through examinations, "the superiority of the best would become evident," Trevelyan and Northcote wrote in an 1854 report to parliament (*Parliamentary Papers* 14). In their formulation, intelligence, a passive object that "become[s] evident" through outside evaluation, seems to cancel labor. It is not enacted or even experienced by the person so much as harbored within him—possessed. According to Hope, the "decisive moves" enabling this view of the mind unfolded in the history of statistics:

> [These moves were] first, [a move] from treating deviations about a mean as errors, to an appreciation that those deviations are the reality that requires explanation, and, second, from mathematical transformations which are no more than restatements of the data . . . to statistical models that treat observed variables as "indicators" of underlying, unobserved, "latent" variables or factors. (12)

The differing mental capabilities of individuals, Hope suggests, came to represent themselves as "underlying, 'latent' variables or factors." Intelligence thus emerged as the latent factor distinguishing a mental from a manual class.

Indeed, specific labor or skills come to seem *opposed* to intelligence: "the superiority in technical skill," Macaulay wrote, "is often more than compensated for by the inferiority in *general intelligence*" (qtd. in Hope 9). Opposed to labor ("cramming," "technical skill"), intelligence was more akin to capital, with capital's peculiar combination of passivity and productivity. "Capital," Marx wrote, "appears as a mysteriously self-creating source of interest—the source of its own increase" (*Capital* 1: 384). Both capital and intelligence might be understood as nouns paradoxically possessing the properties of verbs; that is, while capital and intelligence simply "are"—they are effortless in and of themselves—they nonetheless, if properly invested and cultivated, "mysteriously" generate profit and knowledge respectively. While the worker's body is a kind of conduit or vehicle *through which* profit might accrue, the professional's mind generates out of itself its own profitable knowledge. This is precisely the difference between "cramming" and "ability," the distinction that was so crucial for Macaulay. When one crams, one takes information in and moves it out; when one has ability, one constructs knowledge independently.

David Copperfield associates cramming with the scheming Murdstones. Upon taking over the Copperfield household, this pair institutes a regime of lessons in which David must recite the knowledge he was to have acquired the previous day. Such a system of knowledge consumption—a kind of planned obsolescence in which knowledge has a twenty-four-hour shelf-life—fails miserably:

> I begin to feel the words that I have been at infinite pains to get into my head, all sliding away. . . . I hand the first book to my mother. Perhaps it is a grammar, perhaps a history or geography. I take a last drowning look at the page as I give it into her hand, and start off aloud at a racing pace while I have got it fresh. I trip over a word. (51)

The knowledge itself is incidental ("perhaps it is a grammar, perhaps a history or geography"); what is crucial is David's (in)capacity to use his mind less as a productive force than as a way station, something to hold a commodity only until it is time to ship it out. Knowledge is figured as *outside*—first, as something to "get into" one's head; and, second, as an object placed not only outside but in opposition to oneself—hurdles one is more likely to trip over than surmount.

David's old friend Mr. Micawber offers an alternative approach to the development of the young mind. When he learns that David no longer works in a factory but instead has become a "pupil," Mr. Micawber declares: "'A mind like my friend Copperfield's, does not require that cultivation which, without his knowledge of men and things, it would require, still it is a soil teeming with latent vegetables—in short . . . it is an intellect capable of getting up the classics'" (245). While we would hardly want to trust Mr. Micawber's assessment of his own mind, at this moment, his view of David's possesses the ring of truth. (Indeed, Mr. Micawber's problem is not so much that he is ever *wrong* but that he is profoundly unable to apply his knowledge to himself: "'My advice is so far worth taking,'" Mr. Micawber tells David at one point, "'that—in short, I have never taken it myself, and am the . . . miserable wretch you behold'" [166].) In Mr. Micawber's formulation, a mind is "cultivated"; it nurtures and develops the seeds of knowledge which are already there, "teeming" and "latent." A person's history is simply the inevitable coming to fruition of what the mind originally contained. Already having experienced so much of "men and things," David's mind, of course, needs less cultivation than others. Still, Mr. Micawber says, if David is already wise in the ways of the world, his is a mind capable of being wise on an array of subjects. The quality of mind, its ability to take on a number of studies, is more important than any specific quantity of information. Here we have Macaulay's general intelligence figured as a rich soil. The difference between the Murdstonian and the Micawberian (or Macaulayan) approaches is the difference between intelligence understood as knowledge taken in and spit out and intelligence understood as a far-ranging, inherent capacity that transcends and also, insofar as the mind holds history in advance, collapses time.

This difference, the novel argues, may also be recognized through the difference between commodities, things bought and sold, and capital, something capable of magically extending itself to reap repeated profits. It is no accident, for example, that while in Mr. Micawber's scenario David's mind yields a crop of classics, with the Murdstones it begins to drown ("a last drowning look at the page" [51]) only to surface with unwanted commodities: "I can't think about the lesson. I think of the number of yards of net in Miss Murdstone's cap, or of the price of Mr. Murdstone's dressing gown, or any such ridiculous problem that I have no business with, and don't want to have anything at all to do with" (51). Such a commodifying approach to knowledge, Dickens suggests here, is never profitable. It is, in fact, more likely to generate debt, as "[mother] shuts the book, and lays it by as an arrear to be worked out when my other tasks are done" (51). By contrast, it is significant that when, as mentioned above, David distinguishes himself at Salem House, becoming the "exception to the general body," his distinction emerges seamlessly from his power of invention. Claiming that he was "like the Sultana Sheherazade" (88), a woman who pulls out of herself a lifetime of stories, David entertains his peers with countless tales. A mind that can generate something out of nothing or at least very little (in this case, the bits and pieces David remembers from the books he read when he was little) is the prerequisite for general intelligence:

> Whatever I had within me that was romantic and dreamy, was encouraged by so much story-telling in the dark; and in that respect the pursuit may not have been very profitable to me. But the being cherished as a kind of plaything in my room, and the consciousness that this accomplishment of mine was bruited about among the boys, and attracted a good deal of notice to me though I was the youngest there, stimulated me to exertion. In a school carried on by sheer cruelty, whether it is presided over by a dunce or not, there is not likely to be much learnt. I believe our boys were, generally, as ignorant a set as any schoolboys in existence. . . . But my little vanity . . . urged me on somehow . . . and made me, for the time I was there, an exception to the general body. (90)

While his storytelling "may not have been very profitable" in that it encouraged a certain dreaminess, in respect to academic competition it appears to have been very profitable indeed. Though the youngest pupil, David stands out as the "exception" to the general ignorance among his classmates. David links the approbation he receives from his midnight tales to his academic "exertion" and consequent superiority, hardly a necessary link but one made here as if it follows naturally. What his peers mistake for a commodity, "a kind of plaything," we are meant to identify as mental capital, capable of apparently endless returns.

That David's power of invention, the richness of his soil, qualifies him for a higher professional sphere than might be attainable otherwise becomes clear through the opposition the novel creates between invention and copying. Throughout the novel, those characters devoid of David's intellectual resources but too thoroughly middle class to perform physical work engage in what is figured by the novel as a manual form of mental labor: copying. When "simple" (621) Mr. Dick, for example, attempts to write a work of his own, he can go only so far before ruining it with monomaniacal references to the beheading of King Charles I. But when asked to copy documents that "are already drawn up and finished," documents "Mr. Dick has nothing to do with," he succeeds beautifully, copying in an "orderly, business-like manner" (501). He makes an excellent copyist precisely because his mind is not called upon to create anything. As with cramming, he simply moves words from one spot to another.[10] This depiction of copying is repeated later in the novel with Dora. After David attempts to "form her mind" (660) but gives up when he realizes that her mind is "already formed" (661) and that no amount of knowledge will alter it, Dora chances upon her own way of being useful: she holds his pencils while he writes, giving him a new one as needed. She is literally a way station, a warehouse for pencils awaiting shipment. However, her trafficking in the physical world of objects associates her too closely with manual labor for David perhaps, because pencil-holding "suggest[s] to [him] a new way of pleasing [his] child-wife" (616): having her copy pages from his manuscripts. Yet if Dora upgrades from objects to words, her dearth of mental capital—something one already has or doesn't have, as David learns when he cannot mold her—will keep her from ever being truly productive. Indeed, her ability to *reproduce* in any meaningful or useful way is itself doubtful as David tells us that he only "made a pretence" of needing pages copied (616).

More striking than with either Mr. Dick or Dora, though, is the association of copying with Traddles, a character always to be found "hard at work with his inkstand and papers" (500). Though similar to David in many respects—his energy and discipline, his education, his professional ambition—Traddles lacks David's mental capital. After David has become a successful parliamentary reporter, he tells us that "dear old Traddles has tried the same pursuit but it is not in Traddles's way" (596). Instead, Traddles finds employment with the same newspaper as David in "getting up the facts of dry subjects, to be written about and embellished by more fertile minds" (596). As the novel sees it, research is a kind of rarefied copying, moving facts from textbooks onto the desks of men who can do something more with them. Without the rich soil harbored by David, with a mind less "fertile" than his writing counterparts, the researching Traddles is doomed to reproduce knowledge but never produce it himself.[11] "'I am not a bad compiler,'" Traddles tells David, "'but I have no invention at all; not a particle'" (383).

Ends over Means: Credit and Speculation

Macaulay's insistence that the exam is (or should be) a test of a mind's capital rather than of its capacity to warehouse knowledge did not, of course, prevent many critics of reform from viewing the examination precisely as the commodification of intelligence. Defending the "Public School man" over an imagined (most likely middle-class) beneficiary of the new system, one Victorian wrote:

> The Public School man is felt to have an undoubted superiority,—not necessarily in learning or attainment,—but in qualities *which are beyond price*, facility in using his powers, facility in his behavior to others, facility in ascertaining and keeping his own position, the element of command over other minds. These are qualities which no private system will give, and no system of competitive examination will test. (my emphasis, qtd. in Dyson and Lovelock 17).

In claiming that the "Public School man" possesses "qualities which are beyond price," Moberly implied what later became an explicit critique of the examination system: that the rewarding of prizes, awards, or positions for top examinations created a monetary relationship to knowledge and intelligence; the student no longer appreciated knowledge and intelligence for their own sake. To see this critique as incipient in Moberly's comments, however, is perhaps too generous. More plausibly, Moberly simply played off conventional assumptions about class, locating the aristocrat outside the market and the middle class, with whom the system was associated, squarely within it.[12]

It makes sense, then, that the most sympathetic character who is involved, like David, in what might be called the field of knowledge production, Dr. Strong with his dictionary, is constitutionally unable to finish his project and, thus, never in a position to be paid for it. Dr. Strong's absorption in his work, along with his complete disregard for money (he is forever giving it away, to the great satisfaction of his wife's relatives), contrasts most dramatically with Mr. Micawber, a man whose wife believes him a "genius" (397) but who is so preoccupied with "pecuniary affairs" (398) that he never seems to find the time to work. Indeed, while Dr. Strong avoids the market, Mr. Micawber markets himself, placing an advertisement in "all the papers" in hopes of finding a professional position, selling himself as a man of "great talent," possessing a "variety of qualifications," and ending his advertisement with the imperious injunction, "'*Now* employ me on remunerative terms'" (397). Without first proving himself in any way, Mr. Micawber expects to be hired. Like the Copperfields' servant who prefers stealing time to putting it in, Mr. Micawber expects to receive a high salary without paying his dues.[13] He expects, in short, to be taken on credit. In fact, he takes the very advertisement out on credit. Discussing her husband's inability to pay for the advertisement, Mrs. Micawber suggests that he "raise a certain sum of money—on a bill." "'If no member of my family is possessed of sufficient natural feeling to negotiate that bill . . . [Mr. Micawber] should take that bill into the Money Market, and dispose of it for what he can get,'" she continues; "'I view it, steadily, as an investment . . . which is sure of return'" (398). The one thing the Micawbers can do "steadily" is speculate on future profit.

"Credit creation and disbursement can never be separated from speculation," David Harvey writes; "Credit is, according to Marx, always to be accounted for as 'fictitious capital,' as some kind of money bet on production that does not yet exist" (*Condition of Postmodernity* 107). Harvey coins the phrase "fictitious capital" by drawing on Marx's discussion of land value in *The Eighteenth Brumaire of Louis Bonaparte* and elsewhere. For Marx, since labor could not be the source of land's value, its value emerged in capitalism as a kind of structurally necessary fiction. "Fictitious capital," then, is self-generating profit not "backed up" by any immediate productive activity or "commodity transaction" (*Limits to Capital* 265). This is, in short, as Harvey himself points out, one and the same with what Fredric Jameson and others have called "finance" or "speculative" capitalism, a capitalism predicated on predictions about the future and powered by investment and the stock market rather than by industrial production. A speculative economy might be understood as one characterized by a kind of collapsed temporality in which ends are considered before, or without regard to, means. The measurable economy of industrial capital, structured by the hourly wage, is replaced by what appears to be "profit without production" (*Cultural Turn* 136). Whatever else may be said about speculative capitalism, the important point for my purposes is that in what Jameson calls "the asymmetries of a finance market" (*Cultural Turn* 138) time loses the one-to-one correspondence with money that characterizes it in wage labor. Instead, time is "future oriented."[14] It is put on hold until some unspecified future moment, "until," as Mr. Micawber repeatedly says, "something turns up (which I am, I may say, hourly expecting)" (166).

In *David Copperfield,* the loss of this correspondence registers as a pathology of time. Sending letters to people not after days have passed since he last saw them but seconds, sending out invitations to parties that, when they arrive, "refer to the evening then wearing away" (503), Mr. Micawber cannot match his movements to the appropriate moment. He is forever waiting on time for some installment of money that doesn't come, running from time catching up to him in the form of overdue bills, or manipulating time in order to make money by incurring more debt. Mr. Micawber is stuck in a speculative limbo, imagining "if" but never "when." Upon leaving debtor's prison, he announces, "'I have no doubt I shall, please Heaven, begin to be beforehand with the world, and to live in a perfectly new manner if—in short, anything turns up'" (160). He plans to live "beforehand," facing time rather than running ahead of or behind it, but our confidence in his claim is undone by his "please Heaven," suggesting as it does that his success relies more on chance than on his own efforts, and of course by his ending caveat with which he reverts to his old pattern of anticipation. Speculation, Dickens tells us, is a disease of time.[15] Or, as critic Humphry House put it, speculation in Dickens's novels "is a form of suicide rather than a way of getting on in the world" (59). Thus, a premature (anticipatory) relationship to time has the unintended effect of cutting time off prematurely. Finding himself once again unable to fulfill his "pecuniary obligations," Mr. Micawber reassures David when our protagonist laments that he has no money to lend, "'Copperfield, you are a true friend; but when the worst comes to the worst, no man is without a friend who is possessed of shaving materials'" (248).

In his newspaper advertisement, Mr. Micawber combines the anticipatory temporality of finance capital with an objectification of intelligence in a way that reverberates with the "examination mad"[16] moment in which Dickens writes. That is, just as the advertisement speaks for future labor, the quantification of general intelligence espoused by Macaulay claims to predict accurately a candidate's future success in the civil service. The exam promises to make available ends without recourse to means, disclosing, as Macaulay said, "what men will prove to be in life" (qtd. in Wooldridge 167). To Macaulay, before one actually trained a civil service employee (indeed, Macaulay went so far as to argue that there was no point in having the exam cover information relevant to civil service work), before one witnessed them at work, one could foresee their capabilities. Like the "money bet on production that does not yet exist" defining speculative capital, mental capital presents as a paper bet on labor that does not yet exist. Mental capital—or the concept of general intelligence—implies the exact same collapsed temporality, what Georges Gurvitch calls "time in advance of itself" (qtd. in Harvey 223), in which history does not promise change but the inexorable working out of what was already there in the first place.[17] In this formulation, what is possessed by the mind finds more or less expression (like vegetables with more or less cultivation) but the *person* cannot acquire more mental capital than that with which he begins (as David finds out with Dora). In some palpable way, the time of labor drops out of the equation, and one has the appearance of profit without production—an appearance which, as Mr. Micawber proves time and again, is more mirage than reality.

Making promises on which he cannot make good, the otherwise well-intentioned Mr. Micawber, we begin to realize, is much like the pigeon-pie David serves him one evening. "The pigeon-pie was not bad," David says, "but it was a delusive pie: the crust being like a disappointing head, phrenologically speaking: full of lumps and bumps, with nothing in particular underneath" (391). A faulty phrenological reading—or a false advertisement or, for that matter, a misleading test score—functions in the novel as the mental variant of paper credit; it is fictitious capital artificially inflating a speculative bubble, one bound to collapse just like David's poor pigeon-pie. Up to the moment he sets sail for Australia at the end of the novel, Mr. Micawber is speculating on the future—in this case, on the voyage itself; "'The probability is, all will be found to be exciting, alow and aloft,'" he says; and "with that," David narrates, "he flourished off the contents of his little tin pot, as if he had made the voyage, and had passed a first-class examination before the highest naval authorities" (770). Fittingly, Mr. Micawber behaves as if he were a successful candidate in a civil service examination, and in doing so, he seems to cancel time, believing himself finished with a journey that has only just begun.

At this point we can begin to see why Mr. Micawber's assessment of David's mind—a mind "teeming" with "latent" "vegetables"—is both right and wrong by the novel's estimate. When Macaulay and others claimed that the examination uncovered the "latent factors" of general intelligence, they mobilized two meanings of "latent." They meant that the exam plumbed the candidate's mental depths in order to ascertain his "true" intelligence rather than staying upon the surface layer of knowledge acquired by cramming; and they meant that the exam could reveal the seeds of the candidate's future, the latent qualities which would invariably manifest over time. *David Copperfield* confirms the idea that "intelligence" somehow precedes and exceeds knowledge, but it hesitates to endorse what we might consider the cancellation of the time of labor implied by both meanings of "latent." In the former, the time-consuming labor of knowledge acquisition is canceled in favor of a mystified concept of essential intelligence; and in the latter, the actual performance of work as *the* test of one's capabilities is by-passed in favor of a literal test, which bets on the quality of labor before it exists. The examination candidate proceeds, we might say then, on *credit.* Like the many species of finance capital (credit, promissory notes, debt, stocks, and "fictitious" capital of all kinds), the examination places a claim on the future. It jumps ahead and imagines an outcome (a successful or unsuccessful career) that has not yet occurred. While Mr. Micawber is right to focus on David's quality of mind (the richness of his soil) rather than, as the Murdstones did, the quantity he can cram, he is wrong to fixate on ends over means. In *partially* endorsing Mr. Micawber, *David Copperfield* attempts to mobilize the cachet of mental capital while simultaneously holding at bay its unsettling link to the anticipatory temporality of speculation.

In sum, the novel must produce a professional who possesses mental capital but who does not speculate or "bank" on that capital, as does Mr. Micawber with his advertisement. David must become a professional writer who draws on his shares of mental capital—not on capital's suspicious future-oriented time but on the reliable clock time of industrial labor. Factory time demands that one master oneself—one's whims, impulses, idiosyncrasies—and so, by an odd paradox, the professional drains the mind from the factory, rendering such labor mechanical work that betrays no sign of the particular self performing it, but then implicitly models himself on this same labor in order to signal his disinterested distance from the self with its needs and desires.[18] However counterintuitive on the face of it, then, *David Copperfield* ennobles David's professional labor by aligning it with labor's most degraded form. "You came out nobly—persevering, self-reliant, self-denying," Aunt Betsy says to David at the novel's end (612).

Means over Ends: Brain Work

Many critics have assumed that the professional (or, more accurately, professionalizing) writer at the mid-nineteenth century would want to distance himself from any association with wage labor. Mary Poovey, for example, argues that the Victorian writer tried to align himself with the "nonalienated" labor of domesticity (101). Another critic, T. W. Heyck, claims that the writing professional sought to identify himself with the figure of the leisured gentleman. Michael Lund, however, argues persuasively that there is one very good reason why the mid-nineteenth-century writer would *want* to be associated with wage labor: a widespread public perception of writers as "idle," the epithet associated with a leisured aristocracy, on the one hand, and an older preindustrial workforce, on the other.[19] An editorial in the *Morning Chronicle*, to take one example among many, declared on January 3, 1850,

"The love of notoriety inherent in mankind, combined with the common distaste for continuous or unexciting labor, will always attract an undue number of recruits from other employments to literature" (qtd. in Lund 17).[20] To counteract such an attitude, writers needed to represent their work not as sporadic bursts of productivity followed by periods of leisure and dissipation but as relatively monotonous and highly laborious. Writers wanted to show that they could work "laboriously and methodically," as David does on his shorthand (519). In other words, they were trying to dissociate themselves from the image of the Romantic genius with his erratic spates of inspiration.

The Romantic writer made sense in an earlier economy, in what E. P. Thompson called in his classic essay "Time, Work-Discipline, and Industrial Capitalism" a piecework economy characterized by "alternate bouts of intense labour and of idleness" (373). In a piecework economy, manufacturers essentially outsourced their labor—that is, they relied upon individuals to make certain products within their homes rather than within a centralized workplace. Such individuals, then, dictated their own methods and schedules—doing things when and if they were inclined and interrupting their labor frequently. With the rise of the modern factory, however, workers shifted from piecework to wage labor, money paid not for a finished product but for time "spent":

> those who are employed experience a distinction between their employer's time and their 'own' time. And the employer must *use* the time of his labour, and see that it is not wasted: not the task but the value of time when reduced to money is dominant. Time is now currency: it is not passed but spent. (359)

Time becomes something "objective," something measurable and outside. It is not experienced subjectively, with work driven by one's personal and irregular inclinations, but is instead, in Georg Lukács's words, "an objectively calculable work-stint that confronts the worker as a fixed and established reality" (88).

The new temporality ushered in by "changes in manufacturing technique which demand . . . a greater exactitude in time-routines" (Thompson 382) matched the needs of writers desiring to depict themselves as successful only through, to use David's phrase, "steady application" (632). By stressing the time-disciplined labor of writing, writers could offset the public's association of writing with idleness. The goal, then, was to create an impression of themselves as prone *not* to the idleness enjoyed by the Romantic genius with his hint of aristocratic leisure or by an undisciplined preindustrial workforce but to the fatigue suffered by workers after prolonged and repetitive labor.

During David's stint as a parliamentary reporter, we see him leave for work at the same time every evening regardless of his health (he is, for example, "made quite unwell" by being "obliged" to leave for work "when dinner was half over" [605]) and regardless of his boredom with the parliamentary discussions he must report upon ("dreary debates," he sighs [656]). He perfectly exemplifies the "literary man" described by Thackeray in *The History of Pendennis*: "A literary man has often to work for his bread against time, or against his will, or in spite of his health, or of his indolence, of his repugnance on the subject to the subject on which he is called to exert himself, just like any other daily toiler. When you want to make money by Pegasus, (as he must, perhaps, who has no other saleable property), farewell poetry and aerial flights" (380). The writer is equivalent to the manual laborer here: each possesses "no other saleable property" than respectively a mind and a body. If by comparing the writer's mind or imagination with the manual laborer's body, Thackeray commodified what might still have carried Romantic and "transcendent" associations—"poetry and aerial flights"—the important thing to note is that it was a comparison that cut both ways. Though it dangerously implicated the professional in market exchange, it also rescued him by association with earnest, "honest" labor—labor in which the writer could overcome his own subjective resistance ("against his will," his "indolence," his "repugnance") and submit to the discipline of "objective" time (not one's own time but another's—"against time," as Thackeray says). Rhetorically, then, the new mental class must simultaneously oppose (brains versus hands) and identify ("my fellow-labourer," Dickens often hailed literary colleagues) with the manual class. Presenting himself as a kind of mental laborer rather than a spontaneous genius, the professional needed to be disciplined, following the protocols of work in an industrial world where hours of leisure were sharply divided from those of labor and one's reliability was proven when one internalized this fact.

Bemoaning the tedium of his new job in one of the "learned professions," Mr. Micawber says, "'To a man possessed of the higher imaginative powers, the objection to legal studies is the amount of detail they involve. Even in our professional correspondence . . . the mind is not at liberty to soar to any exalted form of expression'" (536). Romantic inspiration is rewritten as the self-aggrandizing rationalization made by those who detest labor, those who expect rewards without having to work for them—those who presume ability ("imaginative powers") speaks for itself. In Mr. Micawber's complaint, we see the conflation of the Romantic writer and the speculator, both of whom, after all, expect to be rewarded for "soar[ing]." Eighteenth- and nineteenth-century writing, Kevin McLaughlin points out, everywhere produces a "figurative association of credit with flight" (176); "the commerce and industry of this country," Adam Smith wrote, for example, "cannot be altogether so secure . . . suspended on the Daedalian wings of paper money" (qtd. in McLaughlin 176). Rejecting both paper money's "Daedalian wings" and the Romantic's "aerial flights," Dickens argues in *David Copperfield* that genius cannot be taken on credit. It is not possible, David tells us, for "natural or improved ability [to] claim immunity from the companionship of the steady, plain, hard-working qualities, and hope to gain its end" (576). The "fertile" mind revealed by the examination must be coupled with the time-discipline the mechanized factory exemplified.

In *The Human Motor*, Anson Rabinbach explains that around the mid-nineteenth century a fascination with "fatigue" began to offset a preoccupation with workers' "idleness." This shift occurred, he argues, because Victorian scientists and political economists began to understand the body as a kind of machine; and in doing so, they moved the laborer from a moral-religious framework into a biomechanical one in which he represented an imperfect machine, one hampered by fatigue. "I never could have done what I have done," David tells us, "without the habits of punctuality, order, and diligence" (576), habits that he learned early in life—presumably in part during his time as a factory worker, as these "habits" reproduce the rhythms of the industrial workplace. Habits are rituals that do not require one's conscious attention; they are, in short, mechanical. "[Victorian] writers on habit," Athena Vrettos tells us, "routinely invoked the language of mechanization and mass production to make their arguments, expressing concern about the blurring boundaries of man, mind, and machine" (404). While this "concern" certainly escalated as the century neared its end, as modernism began to dismiss mass-produced cultural objects as mindless, at mid-century the machine represented in fact a kind of ideal for the laborer, as Rabinbach elucidates, but also for the professional mind, as Lorraine Daston and Peter Galison inform us.

To be properly professional, Daston and Galison argued that the mid-Victorian had to acquire what they call "mechanical objectivity." Asserting that this "form of scientific objectivity emerged only in the mid-nineteenth century and is distinct from earlier [forms]," Daston and Galison explain that "machines were [considered] paragons of certain human virtues": "Chief among these virtues were those associated with work: patient, indefatigable, ever-alert machines would relieve human workers whose attention wandered. . . . Instead of freedom of will, machines offered freedom from will—from the willful interventions that had come to seem the most dangerous aspects of subjectivity" (81–82). To be mechanically objective, one must, with

Thackery, say "farewell to poetry and aerial flights," because these things no longer denote Romantic genius but instead signal an undisciplined mind "whose attention wander[s]," a mind prone to "willful intervention." They must be replaced, as we saw at the start of this chapter, with the biomechanical "punctual discharge" of writerly duties.[21] Consequently, the professional, however amply and necessarily endowed with mental capital, experienced not the soaring of the leisured mind but, much more prosaically, the bouts of fatigue brought on by sustained brain work. By the end of the novel, then, when David happens upon the very doctor who attended his birth, bringing us full circle, we understand Mr. Chillup entirely when inquiring about David's work, one professional to another, he says: "'And this action of the brain now, sir? Don't you find it fatigue you?'" (794)

Means over Ends II: Outmoded vs. Modern Models

With his easy natural ability and varied expertise ("I could not help observing how much Steerforth knew, on an infinite variety of subjects, and of how little account he seemed to make his knowledge" [276]), the aristocratic Steerforth might, according to David, "take a high degree" (276) in his college examinations, but, significantly, he has no intention of taking them. Refusing to participate in the reformed system of open competition, Steerforth belongs to the Romantic version of piecework time. Unlike David who always consults clocks and watches, Steerforth has "nothing to consult but his own humour" (301). And unlike David, who works the long hours of a "carthorse" (519), Steerforth is content with only "fitful uses of [his] powers" (306). Without the self-denying qualities of the objective professional, Steerforth gives rein to precisely "the most dangerous aspects of subjectivity," his willfulness leading, of course, to the downfall of the Peggotty family. If Dickens rather graphically uses Steerforth to rewrite outbursts of inspiration from the signs of genius into the disturbing symptoms of a man unable to control his impulses, it uses Dora similarly, pressing her into service in order to expose the naïveté of the mid-Victorian nostalgia for a piecework economy.

Toward the end of his article, Thompson suggested that a piecework economy is one and the same with a gendered domestic one: in both, work stops and starts according to its own "irregular" rhythms rather than the rhythm of the countinghouse clock. Dora, whose attention constantly wanders ("Dora would pay profound attention, perhaps for five minutes, when she would begin to be dreadfully tired, and would lighten the subject by curling my hair" [614]) and who is nothing if not willful exemplifies an outmoded domestic model, one that will be replaced by the focused and self-denying Agnes. In the home Dora attempts to keep for David, for example, nothing is ever on time. The cook serves dinner after five when they were to have eaten at four; "'Do you think she has any idea of time?'" David asks (604). Upon consulting a cookbook, David finds that joints should be roasted "a quarter of an hour to every pound," but, nonetheless, "the principle always failed us . . . and we never could hit any medium between redness and cinders" (609). As David's professional life progresses like clockwork—"for my success," he informs us, "had steadily increased with my steady application" (632)—the household's very clock regresses: "Dora glanced wistfully at the clock, and hinted that she thought it was too fast. 'On the contrary, my love,' said I, referring to my watch, 'it's a few minutes too slow'" (604). That this temporal chaos is not David's fault is clear. Dora is childishly indifferent to the hour ("glanc[ing] wistfully") or is, when made aware of it, behind it (she thinks it is earlier than it actually is), but David is acutely attuned to precise measurements of time ("a quarter of an hour to every pound," "a few minutes too slow"). The most significant symbol of the couple's incompatibility is, it is fair to say, their vastly different relationships to time, a difference underscored here by the fact that David wears a watch while Dora resorts to the communal clock. Indeed, the very manner in which they consult their respective timekeepers enacts their alienating distance from one another: while David "refer[s]," Dora "glanc[es]."

Dora wants time to slow down (she hopes the clock is "too fast") while Mr. Micawber wants it to speed up (waiting for "something to turn up" which he is "hourly expecting"), but the result is the same. Neither the childish Dora—"'think of me as [your] child-wife'" (613), she begs David—nor the speculating Mr. Micawber can go "before-hand with the world," because neither the child nor the speculator understands real time. "Real time," Jameson tells us, "is . . . objective time; that is to say, the time of objects, a time subject to the measurements to which objects are subject." "Clock time," he continues, "presupposes a peculiar spatial machine—it is the time of a machine, or better still, the time of the machine itself" (*Postmodernism* 76). If the child lives in suspended time—a period before he must begin "on his own account" (145), as Murdstone says before sentencing David to factory work—and the speculator occupies future-oriented time, the laborer aligns himself with clock time. And so, of course, does David, a fact we are assured of as early as the novel's first paragraph: "I record that I was born . . . on a Friday at twelve o'clock at night. It was remarked that the clock began to strike, and I began to cry, simultaneously" (1).

But Dora, for all her "make-belief of housekeeping" (617), does not really live outside of time as a child does. Instead, as the novel makes clear, she lives in a preindustrial past. The manner in which she performs the one work she succeeds in doing, copying pages of David's manuscripts, tells us that she moves in the irregular and subjective time of piecework rather than the systematic, objective time in which the novel places the professional: "The preparations she made for this great work, the aprons she put on, the bibs borrowed from the kitchen to keep off the ink, the time she took, the innumerable stoppages she made to have a laugh with Jip . . . are touching recollections to me, simple as they may appear to other men," David tells us (616–17). Dora takes her time getting ready to work and certainly takes her time doing the work itself, mixing labor and leisure freely. She follows, that is, her own subjective time without worrying about the objective time of others (though predictably David worries, self-consciously commenting on how her behavior "may appear to other men"). It is important that this description of Dora at work is explicitly placed in the past ("touching recollections"), because with her "want of system and management" (659), she is herself an anachronism, exhibiting a mode endearing when looked back upon but patently unsustainable in the present. Literally and figuratively behind time, she is unequipped to survive in a modern domestic economy.

If, as I said above, an industrial world sharply divided hours of leisure from those of labor, those hours nonetheless looked a lot alike. That is, while the domestic and public spheres were distinctly removed from one another in space and time, their *ordering* of space and time followed the same logic. As Monica Feinberg Cohen argues in her discussion of another Dickens novel, "home starts to look professional" with "customs and rituals [that] are no less structured and require no less work than those at the office" (82–83). Treated as a "pet" (574) by her family, Dora fatally mistakes the home for a yard within which to frolic. By contrast, raised as her father's housekeeper, Agnes understands that for women the home is a place of work. While David qualifies for his professional pursuits through education and examinations, Agnes never attends school, because, as she says, "'[My father's] housekeeper must be in his house, you know'" (218). But, as it turns out, keeping her father's home is precisely the kind of schooling Agnes needs to qualify as David's wife. But it is not just training that she requires; she also needs a certain species of capital, an ability to produce something out of virtually nothing. Whereas David's hopes for a "baby-smile upon [Dora's] breast" are "not to be" (664), Agnes populates the end of the novel with a pack of children named after *David Copperfield*'s many characters. If Dora is only able to copy the pages of David's fiction, just as Traddles is only able to research while "more fertile minds" like David's "embellish," Agnes is capable of embellishing fiction (in this case, Dickens's) with some characters of her own.

Thriving in a professional world that combines capital and labor, Agnes represents the endpoint of the novel.[22] She is figured as the final piece of the puzzle which, once attained, completes David's professionalizing trajectory. She also signals the final piece in my argument here, because it is by way of getting to Agnes that David demonstrates most dramatically Dickens's desire to construct a professional who *knows* something yet still, paradoxically, must undergo the labor of learning it—a mind that, in essence, must earn (rather than bank on) the capital already "latent" and "teeming" within it.

The novel articulates Dora's and Agnes's fundamental difference from one another not only through the two characters' differing management of time but also through the difference in *David's* relationship to time during the period before he marries each of them. When David loses his inheritance and cannot expect to marry Dora until he has independently acquired enough money, he attempts to speed up time. He tries to get through the means of earning her as quickly as possible. After telling us that "Dora was the reward, and Dora must be won," David tells us that in focusing on this end, he works himself into "a state of transport":

> I stimulated myself into such a heat, and got so out of breath, that I felt as if I had been earning I don't know how much. In this state, I went into a cottage that I saw was to let. . . . It would do for me and Dora admirably; with a little front garden for Jip to run around in, and bark at the tradespeople through the railings, and a capital room upstairs for my aunt. I came out again, hotter and faster than ever, and dashed up to Highgate at such a rate that I was there an hour too early. (493)

Time and labor are out of sync. Trying to speed up time, the work is no longer commensurate with the wage—though "so out of breath," he has nothing to show for it. This state is only exacerbated by his then dwelling (metaphorically figured by his inspecting a potential *dwelling*) on a future time when he and Dora will be together. Each detail in his speculative fantasy (Jip barking at tradespeople, for example) ratcheting up David's "state of transport," he emerges from the cottage more out of step with time "than ever" and arrives at his destination "an hour early." In trying to "transport" himself to the future, David only finds himself in conflict with the time of others, the objective time by which Highgate appointments are scheduled.

The period before he marries Agnes follows a quite different temporal logic, one of self-renouncing means rather than self-aggrandizing ends.

Indeed, David explicitly *defers* uniting with Agnes. Leaving England with what he calls his "undisciplined heart" (776), David refuses to return for a long period of time. "Some blind reasons," he tells us, "that I had for not returning home—reasons then struggling within me, vainly, for more distinct expression—kept me on my pilgrimage" (777). Whereas David consciously subordinates everything to the end reward of Dora in the earlier section of the novel, here David cannot even articulate the reasons for his pilgrimage. While the reader knows by this time that Agnes represents the "end" of his journey, David himself is not allowed to know that which is nonetheless figured as already "within" him. Settling in a small Switzerland town, he resolves to make no decisions "for three months." He "work[s] early and late, patiently and hard," and when the three months expire, he "resolve[s] to remain away some time longer" (779). During this period, he "beg[ins] to think that I might have set [my heart's] earliest and brightest hopes on Agnes" (780). He refuses, however, to return home, because he knows that "if, at that time, I had been much with her," he would tell her this secret prematurely. Indeed, exercising the same discipline with time in his narrative as he does in his life, he waits even to tell us, his readers, this secret: "I have now recalled all that I think it needful to recall here, of this term of absence—with one reservation. . . . I have desired to keep the most secret current of my mind apart, to the last" (779).

As he continues to ponder his life during this retreat, David decides that he has, in fact, lost Agnes:

> In the beginning of the change that gradually worked in me, when I tried to get a better understanding of myself and be a better man, I did glance, through some indefinite probation to a period when I might possibly hope to cancel the mistaken past, and to be so blessed as to marry her. But, as time wore on, this shadowy prospect faded, and departed from me. (780)

Because the past cannot be retrieved and "correct[ed]" (781), David must live in the present, giving up the "end," Agnes. "The older traditional forms of human activity are," Jameson writes of industrial capitalism, "essentially restructured along the lines of a differentiation between means and ends" ("Reification and Utopia" 130). The laborer concentrates only on the former, his moment on the assembly line, forever deferring the latter, the finished product. "I endeavored," David tells us, "to convert what might have been between myself and Agnes, into a means of making me more self-denying, more resolved, more conscious of myself, and my defects and errors" (781).

But, again, the means-ends logic of modern labor cuts both ways. If the separation of means and ends is precisely what makes us trust that David is "self-denying," that he can deny his own self-interests and work in the interests of others, this same distance between the self and its work is also troublesome. As Jameson describes:

> Surely the emergence of the modern dichotomous view of action [as separable into means and ends] is related to the secularization of action in the modern world in general. . . . Now in the new middle-class culture for the first time people weigh the various activities against each other; what we call private life or individualistic subjectivity, indeed, is precisely the distance that permits them to do so and to hold their professional enterprises at arm's length. ("Vanishing Mediator" 9)

Such holding at arm's length might indicate indifference rather than passionate self-denial. And, so, the logic of self-renunciation must be reconciled with the charismatic logic of the unique self. Therefore, the novel cannot end here. Instead, by realizing that his "earliest" desire was for Agnes, David derives "a better understanding of himself"—a better understanding, significantly, not of who he has become but of who he has been all along. And just as mental capital is harbored within oneself and invariably expressed in time, the "earliest and brightest hopes" lying latent in David's heart are precisely what find cultivation by the end of the novel.

Mirroring the collapsed temporality of the mind whose history is foretold by the outside examination, the "mistaken past" is "cancel[led]" after all, and the story of the novel is rewritten as something that was on some level known in advance—as, indeed, it is on another, more literal, level as well, being an "autobiography."[23] But just as one's "general intelligence" cannot be capitalized on—indeed, it *cannot* be, because, in the act, it converts from mental capital into a false commodity, as when Mr. Micawber markets his faculties—but must be expressed over time in disciplined labor, the intelligence of David's heart, the wise love it has possessed all along in latent form, cannot be experienced by him consciously until it manifests itself in a disciplined heart, a heart that no longer races toward ends but resigns itself to means. Paradoxically, then, David *earns* what he already possesses. He becomes the modern professional, a figure who possesses natural capital but who nonetheless rejects capital's greedily accelerated temporality in order to perform his services in the trustworthy time of industrial labor. Dickens granted his professional (David) disinterestedness not by denying his relationship to the market, as some critics would have it, but by having him adopt an industrial relationship to the market rather than a speculative one.

Just before David marries the "light-headed" Dora, his aunt Betsey exclaims, "'Poor little couple! And so you think you were formed for one another, and are to go through a party-supper table kind of life, like two pretty pieces of confectionery, do you?'" (477). David's near-fatal mistake is in speculating that he knows how he is formed ("you think you were formed for one another?") when, in fact, he cannot know his own mind prematurely, even though it might be known by something outside him—history, external examination, Betsey herself ("'Nobody knows what that man's mind is except myself,'" Betsey says of another character [196]). Later, before he marries Agnes, David foregoes speculation. As a result, despite his claim that by marrying Dora, he thereby "deservedly lost" Agnes (781), the novel permits him to have both. David gets to have his cake—or "pretty piece of confectionery"—and eat it too, and so does Dickens, who succeeded in combining mental capital with the time-disciplined labor it otherwise threatened to cancel out. "Cultural capital," Bourdieu wrote, "manages to combine the prestige of innate property with the merits of acquisition" ("Forms of Capital" 245). One would be hard-pressed to find a better description of Dickens's strategy for inscribing modern professional identity.

CHAPTER THREE

The Professional Paradox:

Competitive Examinations and Anthony Trollope's The Three Clerks

"Calling before us some of the illustrious of the former days, [let us] ask them what they think of us and our doings? Of our astounding progress of intellect? Our march of mind? Our higher tone of morality? Our vast diffusion of education? Our art of choosing the most unfit man by competitive examination?"

—Mr. Gryll, *Gryll Grange* (1861)

"If honest men did not squabble for money, in this wicked world of ours, the dishonest men would get it all; and I do not see that the cause of virtue would be much improved."

—Archdeacon Grantly, *Barchester Towers* (1857)

In the previous two chapters, I discussed how Brontë and Dickens professionalized their protagonists without requiring them to deny the market of economic exchange. In *The Professor* (1847), William Crimsworth demonstrates his professional objectivity by eschewing the market of *sexual* exchange, and in *David Copperfield* (1849–50), Copperfield proves his professionalism by occupying the objective time of manual labor rather than the accelerated time of speculation. Seven years later, when Anthony Trollope went to professionalize his protagonist in *The Three Clerks* (1857), the paradox of the professional—that he must appear indifferent to the market upon which he necessarily relied—had begun to take shape in the Victorian cultural imagination. "Authors are taught that they should disregard payment for their work, and be content to devote their unbought brains to the welfare of the public," reads an infamous passage of Trollope's *Autobiography*; "Brains that are unbought will never serve the public much" (107). Trollope was, and occasionally still is, reviled for comments like this, but his scandalous remarks were not simple provocations. They made up a career-long struggle with the double bind at the heart of professional identity, and *The Three Clerks* was one of his most important attempts to disable that bind. The novel first exposes the professional paradox and then attempts to reverse it by arguing that only when the professional admits self-interest can his judgment be trusted.

I begin this chapter by revisiting the competitive examination. In the last chapter, I explained how mid-nineteenth-century exam culture represented intelligence as a kind of mental capital. Dickens could hold at bay the disturbing implications of this form of capital only by reintroducing the factory: by drawing on his mental capital in factory time, the professional holds on to intelligence's honest objectivity. Here, I consider the debate over competitive examinations at greater length, because it provided Trollope with the context for his intervention in the developing discourse of professionalism. The first third of *The Three Clerks* is organized around a competitive examination, and in this portion of the novel, Trollope illuminates the contradiction underwriting professional identity and simultaneously disqualifies two of his three clerks from the tacit contest over which clerk gets to close the novel as its lone professional. The plot of the remaining third clerk illustrates Trollope's "theory" that self-interest is the prerequisite to disinterest rather than its seedy and denied underside. In conclusion, I show how Trollope's understanding of professional labor in *The Three Clerks* implicitly addresses the conditions of the novel's own production.

Professionalizing the Civil Service: The Debate over the Northcote-Trevelyan Proposal

"The professionalization of government," Perkin writes, "was the greatest political achievement of nineteenth-century Britain" (*Origins of Modern English Society* 270). Perkin locates this achievement in the "great social and administrative reforms"—more specifically, the Reform Acts, which extended the franchise and Civil Service reforms beginning in 1854 and culminated in 1870 in the implementation of open competitive examinations for all Civil Service positions. While the former, social reform, has received extensive treatment by a number of disciplines, the story of administrative reform is relatively unknown outside the circles of governmental history. Yet the changes experienced by the Civil Service in the mid-Victorian period are what ultimately enabled a professional ideology to differentiate itself from a market one, a development that, in turn, made possible the rise of the welfare state. "It was chiefly in the civil servants . . . that the professional ideal began to diverge from the entrepreneurial," Perkin writes (*Origins of Modern English Society* 428). While the latter ideal "was satisfied by the minimal, regulatory, decentralized *laissez-faire* State of Victorian theory," it was the professional ideal that would "press on towards the expanding, centralized, interventionalist State of Victorian practice" (321).

I have argued elsewhere that Dickens's *A Tale of Two Cities* (1859), published only two years after *The Three Clerks,* is the text which best etches the requirement that the professional disavow self-interest onto the cultural imagination (Ruth, "Self-Sacrificing Professional"). Sydney Carton proves his disinterest—and reforms himself and his profession—only by refusing, in the starkest of possible terms, to profit from his services. Watching the debate over the competitive exam unfold in parliament and various periodicals, it is as if we see this principle of professionalism in the act of forming. In arguing over whether competitive examinations would identify the right or wrong man, pundits simultaneously brought the professional into being by giving him a unique and, in a sense, impossible position in the socioeconomic order.

The story of the competitive examination begins with the Northcote-Trevelyan Report of 1854—the paper Noel Annan called the intellectual aristocracy's "Bill of Rights" (247). It proposed replacing a patronage-driven system of recruiting young men into service with a system of selection and promotion through open competitive examination.[1] Sir Stafford Northcote and Sir Charles Trevelyan wrote:

> It would be natural to expect that so important a profession would attract into its ranks the ablest and most ambitious of the youth of the country. . . . Such, however, is by no means the case. Admission into the Civil Service is indeed eagerly sought after, but it is for the unambitious, and the indolent or incapable, that it is chiefly desired. Those whose abilities do not warrant an expectation that they will succeed in the open professions, where they must encounter the competition of their contemporaries, and those whom indolence of temperament or physical infirmities unfit for active exertions, are placed in the Civil Service, where they may obtain an honourable livelihood with little labour, and with no risk. (*Parliamentary Papers* 4)

Open competitive examinations would stock the service, they claimed, with intelligent, capable men. Setting the terms with which Victorians would perceive the new knowledge class that increasingly managed them, the debate triggered by the proposal facilitated "the growing domination in the governors and administrators themselves of the entrepreneurial by the professional ideal" (Perkin, *Origins of Modern English Society* 325). Over the course of the debate, a dialectic emerged: through the criticism of patronage and corruption from the vantage-point of the entrepreneurial ideal, and then through the criticism of the market ideal from the more service-oriented standpoint of the gentlemanly ideal, a new professional ideal came into being.

The debate raged inside parliament and outside in the pages of such journals as *Cornhill Magazine* and *Fortnightly Review.* Even Queen Victoria weighed in, at least in her private letters. On February 7, 1854, she wrote Prime Minister Gladstone to confess "considerable misgivings" (27). The Queen worried that the exam would draw a lower class of servant without the "moral character" possessed by those admitted under the patronage system (27). Her concern was echoed by many of the periodical writers. "The object [of the reform] in point of fact," one *Quarterly Review* author said, as if exposing a conspiracy, "is to turn the 16,000 places in the civil service of this empire into so many places and exhibitions for poor scholars" (qtd. in Mueller 195). If there was a conspiracy, it was precisely the opposite of the one imagined here. The exam may have given the appearance that the Civil Service was throwing the doors open to an intellectually entrepreneurial contingent of the lower bourgeoisie, but it was actually designed to favor those who studied at Oxford and Cambridge.[2] In fact, it is a bit of an oversimplification, but one that allows us to understand better the simultaneous problem and opportunity the exam posed, to say that the proposal's opponents and proponents alike wanted much the same thing—to redeem the increasingly discredited Civil Service and develop for it an aura of modern professionalism. They fundamentally disagreed, however, about the exam's ability to deliver this.

Reformers wanted the exam to make intellectual labor visible as a kind of mental capital so that it could be objectively assessed, but critics claimed, in doing so, the exam risked devaluing the very thing whose value it was trying to determine. Opponents quickly put proponents on the defensive by setting up an opposition that proved irresistible. They opposed the disinterested, thoughtful man who would refuse to treat knowledge like a commodity by sitting for an exam but who would make, nonetheless, the most worthy civil servant to the "crammer," a hack who treats knowledge and his own brains like commodities and who, cramming for the exam, might win the competition but would surely fail as a state servant. An 1861 *Cornhill* essay complained of this "second-rate" man who profits from cramming: "Any definite test, measurable by marks, will be satisfied by a man of this kind infinitely better than by a man who really thinks about what is told him, and even about some things which are not told him. . . . In short, a useful hack is better to drive than a thoroughbred horse" (697–98). Within a few lines, however, the hack indiscriminately laboring converts into the crammer indiscriminately consuming: the candidate, we learn, "swallows *pêle-mêle* [a] heterogeneous mass of theories and extracts" (698).

Another *Cornhill* essay took this rhetorical tactic a step further, leaving the inferior but successful exam-taker outside both mechanical production and mindless consumption, an emblem of the pure act of exchange:

> A man who beats everyone else hopelessly in examinations has almost always the same set of qualities. He goes quietly through the routine prescribed to him without turning to the right hand or the left, or allowing his attention to be diverted to any collateral subject whatever. Any definite piece of knowledge can be put in his head as neatly as if it were a bandbox, and he can always reproduce it in as perfect a state as a lady's bonnet when it comes out of the bandbox. (697)

We have first an image of rational labor—the student single-mindedly going about his routine—the routine, though, is not of his making but has been "prescribed to him." He is more like a machine than a person, a member of what another article called the "race of mechanically driven examinees" (846). But, as soon as the image of mechanical production appears, it is canceled by one of feminine consumption: the candidate as a hatbox. In either case, he is not an agent: the "definite piece of knowledge" is "put in his head" and although he is briefly attributed agency, it is to reproduce not to produce and even then it is immediately taken away again—the knowledge simply "comes out of the bandbox." Whereas Northcote and Trevelyan attempted to gain support for their proposal by rhetorically opposing the servant's idle consumption—he is the "fool of the family" feeding off the state, in Trevelyan's opinion (qtd. in Hughes 72)—to his efficient production through open competition, critics depicted the exam as soliciting a form of mechanical labor that would return the Service to the realm of frivolous consumption. "Civil Service Examinations," sneered the *Financial Reformer*, "are the prettiest things of this kind that we have seen for some time" (qtd. in Mueller 119).

"The school system," Bourdieu wrote, "present[ed] the 'moment of truth' of the examination as its own objective reality" (*Reproduction in Education* 159). The exam is a highly unstable signifier of objectivity, however, because its condensation of time into one moment seemingly vulnerable to "the evils of cramming" (Sayce 697) makes it prey to charges that it is an unreliable instrument at best and one that corrupts what it claims to measure at worst. A distance must be traveled and time must pass for cultural capital to convert into economic capital. Seeming to collapse this distance in its immediacy, the exam commodifies what it aims to consecrate, buying the man who, retroactively, becomes the kind of man who can be bought. As Bourdieu speculated of the professional's cultural capital, "How can this capital so closely linked to the person be bought without buying the person and so losing the very effect of legitimation which presupposes the dissimulation of dependence?" ("Forms of Capital" 248)

In contrast to the crammer, critics posed the "disinterested student" who "occup[ies] his leisure with other subjects than those required by the examination-statute, and follow[s] up some bent of [his] own" (Sayce 836). Disinterest is, in a sense, made possible only *through* leisure—"the free play of the mind on all subjects which it touches," as Matthew Arnold would write a few years later (1057). Unlike the consumption of the crammer, this is a good form of consumption that enables, in turn, real production, real learning. But it is production and consumption that resemble neither because the two take place simultaneously, foregoing the moment of exchange. The good student's intellectual labor is figured as work that is not really work: it is a kind of occupation—learning *occupies* his leisure—but one structurally removed from production destined for the market—learning occupies his *leisure.*

In representing the work of the intellect as simultaneous work and play, production and consumption, opponents implicitly drew on the aesthetic tradition. To distinguish the artwork from the commodity, Kant removed artistic labor from the appearance of material necessity by changing it into play. And just as Kant found himself relying on nature to represent this seemingly impossible entity, the thing produced without labor, so too critics of the exam analogized intellectual labor to nature. "The more important qualities," wrote one opponent, "are in their very nature incapable of being brought to a definite test. It would be absurd to try to express in marks the difference between a good judge and a bad one, as to try to measure a mountain with a two-foot rule" (Anonymous 707). Constructing an analogy that demanded intellectual labor be represented as a visible object, something placing it in the realm of the potentially commodifiable, the writer avoided this possibility by retreating from the man-made world into the sublime. The same reasoning that moved Kant to ground aesthetic value in nature operated to underwrite intellectual value here. Because "[natural] beauty never passes through the market, and can never be assigned a value in exchange," it could appear to ground an extra-economic model of value (Guillory, *Cultural Capital* 319).

Like opponents, supporters of the proposal also assumed that "the quality of the mind" is something entirely different from "the quantity of the stores with which it [is] furnished" (Morison 538), but they claimed the exam would not reward those who crammed for it but rather those in whom it detected something preexistent, something independent of the exam itself. Through examinations, Northcote and Trevelyan wrote, "the superiority of the best would become evident" (14). Intelligence, a passive object that "become[s] evident" through outside evaluation, seems to cancel labor. It is not enacted or even experienced by the person so much as harbored within him—possessed. If conducted correctly, one writer opined, the exam "place[s] the [examinee] on a standard table in such a position that if it were possible from a physical examination of his brain to judge of his brain capacity, the results of the two methods would coincide" ("Competitive Examinations" 417). The proponents defended the exam, then, by creating a figurative candidate who could hardly be accused of self-interested cramming, because *he* is bypassed as his capacity is illuminated like an x-rayed bone. By 1875, such a distinction between innate capacity and mere learning would apparently acquire enough cultural purchase that *Fortnightly Review* deemed it necessary to devote an entire article to challenging the "antithesis between genius and learning, as if the one almost necessarily excluded the other" (Morison 538).

It might be argued, though, that the exam's champions resurrected the problem when they thought they were laying it to rest. That is, in depicting the examination candidate as a disinterested spectator in order to repel the charge of craven cramming, defenders of the exam reified the candidate's capacities, characterizing them as if they were discrete and external to the candidate himself. "The problems of consciousness arising from wage-labour were repeated in the ruling class," Lukács wrote in *History and Class Consciousness*; "The specialized 'virtuoso,' the vendor of his objectified and reified faculties, does not just become the [passive] observer of society; he also lapses into a contemplative attitude *vis-à-vis* the workings of his own objectified and reified faculties" (100). When the "workings" of one's mind become "objectified" in the form of "faculties," one becomes a "vendor," and thus, presumably, not fundamentally different from the laborer selling labor-power. The problem for mental capital, then, is that what is the primary mechanism to attribute and restrict it—the exam—also potentially denatures it. Regulating the professional monopoly of intelligence, the exam places intelligence within a grid of equivalencies, assigning it an exchange value. At the moment of its convertibility into a relative value, the threat arises that such property will not turn into a kind of capital but will commodify its owner.

The professional class is a class whose intelligence ideally resembles capital more than it does labor but whose extra-economic rationale disallows its easy assimilation into the capitalist class. "Cultural capital," John Guillory writes, "is certainly a species of symbolic capital generally, but it is a form of symbolic capital certifiable by objective mechanisms" ("Bourdieu's Refusal" 15). The professional's cultural capital accrues through examination or other forms of external recognition, but it is a form of symbolic capital, and symbolic capital cannot accrue unless it *refuses* any externally derived recognition (money, awards, etc.). The professional paradox derives from the professional's reliance on a form of capital that must be simultaneously visible (objective) and invisible (subjective), valuable and invaluable. It must be visible not in the form of labor but rather in the form of quantified property so that it may freely circulate on the market and so that, in the case of the Civil Service, it may provide an ostensibly objective counterpoint to patronage. Yet at the same time, to avoid the degradation of commodification, it must be invisible—defined negatively rather than positively, by its resistance to measurement and its distance from the market. The debate outlined the contradiction that sustains the professional class even as it renders professional identity particularly precarious—the contradiction of a class functionally inside but symbolically outside the market.

Perhaps nothing demonstrated Trollope's desire to inhabit the identity of the professional seamlessly more than his speech at a Royal Literary Fund function in 1861. "I have risen on behalf of Writers of Fiction to thank you for the honour which you have done them in drinking their health, and in drinking this toast to them as a distinct and established branch of a distinct and established profession," he said, adding in the next sentence, "I cannot sit down without professing my belief that the branch of the profession of literature is distinct, and is established, and is useful and is ornamental"; and, then, only a few sentences later: "I say that branch of the profession to which I belong is a useful as well as an ornamental branch" (qtd. in Super 320). It is as if saying it could make it so. Yet, however much Trollope wished to belong to a profession and to identify as a professional, he could never reconcile himself to the constitutive contradiction of professional identity, the contradiction that called upon him to disavow the one thing he perhaps coveted even more than a professional persona—a thriving market for his "services."

The Three Clerks: Sociology in Disguise

As Pierre Bourdieu has argued of *Sentimental Education* (1869), *The Three Clerks* can be read as sociology-in-disguise, so accurate is its illustration of social reproduction. Flaubert's *Sentimental Education* isolates a group of students and unfolds the trajectory each takes as he transitions to adulthood and becomes a relative success or failure in life. From a position of apparent equality, these characters are launched, Bourdieu says, "like particles into a force-field" and "the dispositions, that is to say, the ensemble of incorporated properties, including elegance, facility of expression or even beauty, and capital in its diverse forms—economic, cultural, social—constitute the trumps which will dictate both the manner of playing and success in the game" (*Rules of Art* 10). The main character Frederic has all the trumps he needs but in fatally equivalent portions. He is not determined in one career path or another by his set of embodied and economic capital but rather is balanced between the disinterested world of art and the acquisitive world of politics and business. Waffling between the two, he is destined to fail in both—a poster-child for what Bourdieu calls "determined indeterminacy" (*Rules of Art* 4). *The Three Clerks* also launches its characters from a position of virtual equality. Harry, Alaric, and Charley have all begun careers in the Civil Service and all socialize with the same family, a clergyman's widow and her three daughters. The tale follows these three men as they graduate to adulthood, each establishing, or failing to establish, a vocation and each courting and then marrying one of the daughters (Gertrude, Linda, or Katie).

Flaubert created a novel that manages to illustrate the determination of indeterminacy while recapitulating this indeterminacy—a kind of neutrality among, or equidistance from, established positions—at the level of the sentence, exuding aesthetic disinterest. According to Bourdieu, by occupying "that neutral place where one can soar above groups and their conflicts" (*Rules of Art* 26), Flaubert mapped the logic of symbolic capital. To explain briefly, for Bourdieu, a general economy of practices extends from the economic field at one end to the field of cultural production at the other. Those figures with primarily economic capital, like industrial or finance-capitalists, cluster at one end while those relying largely on what Bourdieu calls cultural and symbolic capital, like the professional and a step further, the artist, occupy the other. These latter must do what they do without regard for the market ("Field of Cultural Production" 321). The professional must repress his own interests in his attendance on others while the artist must subordinate personal desires in his commitment to art for art's sake. "'Symbolic capital' is to be understood," he writes, "as economic or political capital that is disavowed, mis-recognized, and thereby recognized, hence legitimate, a 'credit' which is, under certain conditions, and always in the long run, capable of assuring 'economic profits'" (*Rules of Art* 142). The field of cultural production reproduces this dynamic within itself by commercial art that satisfies extrinsic expectations and garners immediate profit, on one end, and avante-garde art that strives to satisfy only the intrinsic demands of the art itself and collects its profit either not at all or only after considerable delay, on the other.

However similar their sociological experiments, *Sentimental Education* and *The Three Clerks* occupy opposite ends of the field of cultural production. Whereas Flaubert's avant-garde *Sentimental Education* everywhere implies that the only readers qualified to judge it are Flaubert's own peers, if not Flaubert alone—that, in Bourdieu's terms, the novel belongs to the field of restricted production—Trollope's resolutely bourgeois *The Three Clerks* targets a larger readership, taking up a position in the field of general production. While Flaubert flaunted his refusal to cater to the market requirements of a realist novel, thereby enacting the modern principle of aesthetic autonomy by his formal exactitude, Trollope flaunted his *submission* to preexisting expectations, thereby creating an ironic distance of his own. This difference in form between the two novels finds its reflection in the kind of sociology each might be said to practice. Flaubert's dissection of mid-century France makes any participation in its culture appear invariably contaminated and contemptible, while Trollope's novels seem to forgive their characters' inevitable complicity, suggesting that there is more potential for virtue in doing as others do around you than there is in high-minded abstention.

Bourdieu, the son of a postman, and Trollope, a postman himself, pay particular attention to spatial coordinates—where individuals originate and where they end up. Indeed, the very first paragraphs of *The Three Clerks* consist of a fairly elaborate mapping of the social geography of the Civil Service. Trollope details the location, facades, and relative prestige of various offices, beginning with what is "popularly called the Weights and Measures" (8). This "well-conducted" office with its "handsome edifice" is clearly the most important branch of the service. "All material intercourse between man and man must be regulated, either justly or unjustly, by weights and measures," Trollope explains, "and as we of all people depend most on such material intercourse, our weights and measures should to us be a source of never-ending concern" (8). Trollope grows facetious as he continues—"And then the question of the decimal coinage! is it not in these days of paramount importance?"—but that does not change the fact that this one sentence in the novel's third paragraph establishes the logic that will govern the text as a whole. Having arranged a set of equivalents—three young men all starting careers in the same field and wooing sisters—the novel will proceed to differentiate them, explaining how various "weights and measures" determine whether they succeed or fail.

Harry Norman and Alaric Tudor are clerks in the Office of Weights and Measures. Issuing from a landed family, Harry Norman has all the obvious advantages—money, manners, looks, intelligence, a proper education, access to society—but he lacks the will to succeed (his "fault," according to the narrator, is that he is "somewhat shy and reserved . . . among men" [5]). The son of a deceased, bankrupted cavalry officer, Alaric Tudor has no economic capital, dubious cultural capital ("his education had been very miscellaneous"[7]), but boasts a hypertrophied will to succeed ("He was ambitious; and lived with the steady aim of making the most of such advantages as fate and fortune had put in his way" [7]). Alaric's cousin Charley Tudor clerks in the Office of Internal Navigation, a lowly and soon-to-be-obsolete office. The son of a clergyman, Charley has no economic capital, a little cultural capital, and a moderate will to succeed. He is the third term placed between Harry's disinterest and Alaric's overweening ambition. Not so different from Flaubert's Frederic, Charley has a little bit of everything but not a lot of anything. He is not clearly determined in one direction or another but rather is "easily malleable, . . . tak[ing] at once the full impression of the stamp to which he [i]s subjected" (55). But where Frederic's blankness, the relative openness of his undetermined trajectory, is his downfall, Charley's malleability is his trump card. According to Trollope, only by doing as others do—internalizing their protocols and norms, accepting their weights and measures—will one succeed.

The critical turning point in the plot takes the form of a competitive examination between Harry and Alaric. Presided over by examination-mad Mr. Hardlines (based on Sir Charles Trevelyan), Weights and Measures conducts a competitive examination for an important promotion. At first, it appears that Harry and Alaric each embody one side of the opposition sketched by the anti-exam pundits. We have a "free, generous intelligence" (*Parliamentary Papers* 19) set against a mind that acquires knowledge "for what it will fetch" (Sayce 836). "True" Harry withdraws from the competition, and "schem[ing]" Alaric emerges the victor (5, 19). We are not to be surprised by this outcome, considering what we already know about Alaric—that he "was perhaps not superior to Norman in point of intellect; but he was infinitely superior in having early acquired a knowledge of how best to use such intellect as he had" (7–8) and that he "got the best of [every] bargain" (8). Alaric hardly stops to enjoy his success. Instead, calling to mind one parliamentary member's concern that the examination would produce men "too *conceited* for the duties required of them" (*Parliamentary Papers* 61), he is "already beginning to think that this Weights and Measures should only be a stepping-stone to him" (131). What one contemporary reviewer called Alaric's "ill-regulated ambition" (Review in *Spectator* 59) will later lead him to use government information for private gain, setting off a series of deceits which land him not in the parliamentary office he imagines for himself but in prison. Having commodified one's brains, the examination proceeds to turn one, the novel suggests, into a market agent rather than the loyal Crown servant the exam was meant to identify. "He knew his own value," Trollope writes of Alaric, "and did not fear but that he should find a price for it in some of the world's markets" (381).

The exam does not reward the superior man but the man who knows how to use his brain as a marketable commodity. In this, Trollope appears to agree with the opponents of the proposal—the exam, as the *Fortnightly Review* piece put it, "traffics in brains" (Sayce 844). But Alaric is not the mechanically driven, cramming candidate. (Another unfortunate fills that role: "[Mr. A. Minusex] had so crammed himself with knowledge that his mind—like the gourmand's stomach—had broken down under the effort, and he was now sobbing out algebraic positions under his counterpane" (126–27).) Alaric does not prepare for the exam. He does not treat his brain like a warehouse to be stocked for the exam but rather like stock itself, something to be speculated upon. According to Trollope, the problem with the exam is not that it defiles professionalism by assigning it an exchange value. The problem is rather that the exchange value applies not to professional labor already performed but to labor that has yet to exist. Allegedly gauging one's general capacity and, thus, predicting the worth of one's future labors, the exam acts as a form of speculation. Embodying this logic, Alaric says to himself in anticipation of the exam, "Education is nothing—mind, mind is everything" (76). Appropriately enough, then, Trollope turns Alaric into an obsessive stock-jobber, constantly trading with his insider knowledge. (Indeed, the novel portrays Alaric as so consistently compulsive in his speculations that he speculates in his personal as well as his professional life; at one point, for instance, he considers it useful to "raise an interest in Linda's heart" [55]).

If we were dealing with anyone but Trollope, the novel would have ended there, consigning Alaric to prison while catapulting the deserving Harry Norman to great heights in another, perhaps more prestigious profession. But, in fact, the novel shuts the door on Harry as firmly as it does on Alaric, retiring him to his family estate where he occupies a place literally rather than symbolically outside the market. Trollope reproduces the anti-exam logic, but in part so that he can expose its illogic—its mystification of the fact that only those originally possessing economic capital can claim uncommodified mental capital. Harry can afford to be high-minded because he has an independent income. Criticism has tended to take Trollope to task for his romanticized view of the gentleman, but this novel emphatically denies that figure hero status. Harry's withdrawal from the competition is depicted as an unmanly act of cowardice, one that should not surprise the reader, considering that the narrator damned Harry early in the novel by noting that he "prefer[s] the society of ladies to any of the bachelor gaieties of his unmarried acquaintance" (5). The exam, then, shakes out two identities: the businessman and the gentleman—the former claiming autonomy from patronage, the latter enjoying autonomy from the market—neither of whom approximated the professional the Civil Service sought.

Trollope's Unheroic Hero

The Three Clerks' remaining clerk proves his aptness for civil service by being just what the pundits despised: a hack. The advocates of the Northcote-Trevelyan Report wanted a man whose intelligence was detectable by the exam, the critics wanted a man whose disinterested play led him to reject the exam, but neither group wanted a man who was essentially a mental laborer. Proponents and opponents alike heaped scorn upon the man who labors unimaginatively through his routine but this is the very man Trollope makes his hero. Where the anti-exam essayists turned the hack into a consumer, *The Three Clerks* turns its frivolous consumer into a productive, if uninspired, mental laborer who writes bad fiction published serially in cheap papers. "Gay, thoughtless, rollicking" Charley's primary flaw is that he ingests too much of modern life—"A short pilot-coat, and a pipe of tobacco, were soon familiar to him, and he had not been six months in London before he had a house-of-call in a cross lane running between Essex Street and Norfolk Street" (15). The remainder of the novel charts his progress from a slacker civil servant and immoderate man-about-town into a writer with enough discipline to produce rather than consume petty commodities.

Charley starts off the tale at a disadvantage. Without either Alaric's cleverness or Harry's moral superiority, Charley, as one contemporary reviewer noted, "begins in the wildest ways—haunts taverns, consults Jews, and kisses pretty barmaids, utterly regardless of consequences" (Dallas 108). But Trollope turns Charley's bad behavior into the sign of his potential. About the readiness with which Charley picks up the bad habits of his fellow clerks in the Office of Internal Navigation, for example, the narrator says:

> How should it have been otherwise? How can any youth of nineteen or twenty do other than consort himself with the daily companions of his usual avocations? Once and again, in one case among ten thousand, a lad may be found formed of such stuff, that he receives neither the good nor bad impulses of those around him. But such a one is a *lapsus naturae.* He has been born without the proper attributes of youth. (17)

Almost *because* he is so resolutely average in comparison with the other clerks who are either too noble or too ignoble, Charley is the one most likely to succeed. He has no attribute in any impressive degree but he is also "deficient in no proportion of mind necessary to make an estimable man" (17). Like Frederic, there is nothing particularly noteworthy about him, and if he did not get "boisterous" from time to time, we would hardly remember he was there (17). He is, in fact, perfectly suited to prove that professions do not *find* the right man, as Northcote and Trevelyan expected to do with the examination, but must *make* him.

According to Trollope, men act professionally in a system that expects them to do so and that rewards them accordingly, not out of any innate capacity for professionalism. "Assigning someone to a group of superior essence (noblemen as opposed to commoners, men as opposed to women, educated as opposed to uneducated, etc.)," Bourdieu wrote, "causes that person to undergo a subjective transformation that brings about a real transformation likely to bring him closer to the assigned definition" (*State Nobility* 112). Or, as Friedson comments, "the producers themselves have to be produced" (32). Trollope writes, "Had [Charley] gone into the Weights and Measures . . . he would have worked without a groan from ten till five, and have become as good a model as the best of them" (18). This hypothesis is duly proven, as are all the narrator's hypotheses in this novel of "almost ritualistic predictability" (Shuman, *Pedagogical* 89). Charley does manage to make it into Weights and Measures, though he escapes examination. Instead, what the narrator sarcastically calls his "heart-rending tales" make his ascendance of the Civil Service's ranks possible (534).

Soon after Charley's first story appears in the penny paper *Daily Delight*, the Office of Internal Navigation is dissolved. "Mr. Oldeschole began to set his house in order, hopelessly," writes the narrator of Charley's old boss, "for any such effort the time was gone by" (527). Harry recommends that Charley be given his now-vacated post. Charley is admitted and given a position "equal in seniority and standing as that which he had held at the Navigation, and much higher, of course, in pay" (536). Meddling reformers protest that Charley was "admitted without examination" (536). At a parliament session, they compare Charley to one of the Internal Navigation clerks who was cut adrift altogether. Why, they ask, are the two treated so differently? Passing around a badly scrawled note written by the fired clerk alongside a literary review offering "some half-dozen lines, highly eulogistic" of Charley's first story, one member calls for everyone to compare the two and "'then the House would see whether or no the produce of the Civil Service field had been properly winnowed'" (538). But even if the House endorses Charley, our narrator does not: "Poor Screwy was the goose, and certainly got the sauce best suited to him when he was turned adrift out of the Civil Service. Charley was the gander and fond as I am of him for his many excellent qualities, I am fain to own that justice might fairly have demanded that he be cooked after the same receipt" (536).

At the transition between adolescence and manhood, Bourdieu writes, young men "must enter into one or another of the social games which are socially recognized, and engag[e] in an inaugural investment, both economic and psychological" (*Rules of Art* 13). Charley has a bad track record as a civil servant and his fiction does not indicate any great talent in that sphere either. It is rather the industriousness he exhibits as he writes that matters—the investment he makes is determined not by the aesthetic value of his fiction but by the labor he commits to it. Charley does not need to produce anything remarkable but rather must demonstrate his capacity for disciplined mental labor. Telling in this respect is that the novel's highest praise refers to what Charley is *not* rather than what he *is* when he writes: "At this time Charley was not idle" (533). "Entering a career in Trollope means the formation of a 'disposition' for that very career," Nicholas Dames writes ("Trollope and the Career" 255), and Charley prepares himself for Weights and Measures by developing a disposition for prosaic brainwork.[3] Demonstrating that he has "what the bourgeois call a serious side" (Bourdieu, *Rules of Art* 11)—that he does not suffer from Alaric's conceitedness nor from Harry's impractical loftiness—Charley buckles down to inherit the professional status bequeathed him as the son of a professional. "The vocational process in Trollope," Dames explains, "might be best expressed as the narrative of learning to want what you are in the way of getting" ("Trollope and the Career" 255).

While some Victorian novels blithely reproduced the ideological chiasmus whereby the professional or artistic protagonist cultivates the disinterest that then implicitly earns him those material conditions that in reality make disinterest possible (inheritance, market success, tenure), Charley achieves the relative autonomy of the tenured bureaucrat not through any act of disinterested devotion to the state but instead through the hack's refusal to disregard payment and the success he subsequently enjoys. As his editor holds forth on possible literary topics for the young author, we learn that "the author himself, with base mind, was thinking how much he should be paid for his past labours" (535). When Charley does ask his editor about payment, saying that "he understood that there was so much per sheet, or something of that sort" (535), the editor explains that, at the moment, payment is out of the question—Charley must "have the courage . . . to work through with the *Daily Delight* till it had achieved its promised popularity" (535). Refusing to *defer* payment, refusing the logic by which cultural capital converts to economic form only after a distance is traveled and time passed, Charley decides to peddle his wares elsewhere. "'You will find it very difficult to fly if you tie the whole weight of the *Daily Delight* under your wings,'" a friend tells him; "So Charley prepared himself for solitary soaring" (535). If Frederic in *Sentimental Education* fails because he cannot commit to one game, then Charley succeeds in part because he refuses to be played.

If Flaubert mapped the field of cultural production, then he also submitted to its implicit rules. Conversely, Trollope attempted to escape those rules by making them explicit, specifically the rule requiring one to disavow material interest in favor of a heroic commitment to art or, in the professional's case, to "service." By acting out of honest self-interest rather than pretending to some higher nobility of purpose, Charley succeeds.[4] According to Trollope, it was unreasonable and naïve to expect one to work disinterestedly, without rewards, and, so long as one did an honest day's work, no shame needed to attach to professional or artistic self-interest. "No work can be fairly done but by routine," Trollope writes, and Charley signals his submission to bureaucratic routine by submitting to the mechanics of serial publication, a form in which his writing comes out "bit by bit" (534). In the sphere of arts and letters where one most expects to find disinterested play or flights of self-aggrandizing fancy, Trollope places the kind of dutiful, plodding labor the civil servant must prove himself capable of performing. "Fortunately," Secretary of the Board of Trade James Booth wrote in response to the Northcote-Trevelyan Report, "commanding talents, or extensive acquirements in any great number are not required." He continued:

> They would, in fact, be misplaced in almost every department of the Government. It is rather steady and persevering devotion to the every day business of the department that is to be desired: and it is one of the chief objections to your system of competition that from the over-education of clerks, accompanied probably by a corresponding amount of self-estimation, there would, looking at the character of the work to be done,

> and the slow rate of promotion, be much disappointment and dissatisfaction with their work, attended probably as a general consequence, with listlessness and indolence. (*Parliamentary Papers* 134)

Implying much the same thing, Lord Ellenborough admonished reformers, "Recollect that the civil servant in England is a clerk" (qtd. in Reader 95).

As for the reformers, there is no danger in their having abandoned their examination system when they promoted Charley, because, again, the Civil Service does not so much *identify* as it does *produce* the right man. Disinterest, Trollope suggests, is a function of institutional circumstances and expectations, not moral character. He shifts the emphasis from individual motivation to the structure of the field, much like sociologist Talcott Parsons a half-century later and Bourdieu a half-century after Parsons. "The conflict is not generally a simple one between the actor's self-interest and his altruistic regard for others or for ideals," Parsons wrote of the paradox of the professional, "but between different components of the normally unified goal of 'success'" (58). What are the steps—the norms and values one must internalize, the dispositions one must cultivate—to succeed in any given field? Being a man who naturally desires the esteem of those around him, Charley quickly internalizes the values of the Weights and Measures and behaves accordingly. If he was a very bad servant when relegated to the idle and useless Internal Navigation Office, he is a splendid one once he is placed "among the stern morals and hard work of the Weights and Measures" (118), if only because "Charley led a busy life; and as men who have really something to do have seldom time to get into much mischief, he had been peculiarly moral and respectable" (496).

If Harry's attenuated will to succeed leads him to abandon his career and Alaric's swollen one makes him mismanage his, this is only to be expected. Both the under- and overdeveloped will stem from the characters' stock of capital, embodied and economic, which cause them to inherit seamlessly the positions of their fathers—Harry reproducing the gentility of his father's life, Alaric reproducing the disreputable vicissitudes of *his* father's. Charley's father is a clergyman, a man belonging to one of the ancient, gentlemanly professions, and the professional too begets a professional. Charley, however, is a modern professional, and if he looks more like a manual laborer than he does like the genteel professional man of the past, it is because Trollope refuses to define the professional by his devotion to disinterested service. Attempting to escape the ideological double bind stipulating that the professional be materially within but symbolically removed from the market, Trollope reduces intellectual labor to labor's simplest form. Pure labor pretends to be nothing other than what it is. It is as if only by adopting the most transparent system of "weights and measures"—the simplest, and, thus, most reliable unit of value—can one act with integrity and also, to borrow a phrase from the novel, "get on in the world" (42).

In his essay "The Civil Service as a Profession," first given as a presentation to his own (postal) branch of the service, then published in *Cornhill* in 1861, Trollope claimed that his goal was to "prove that the Civil Service may be made as noble, as independent, and as free a profession as the bar or church; as arms or medicine" (214). For Trollope, that independence is conferred when one imagines oneself within the apparently straightforward space of the market:

> For every half-crown that they receive, let [civil servants] be careful to give work to the value of three and sixpence, and then let them not care a straw for any man. He who so arranges his weights and measures, never does care a straw for any man. There is no difficulty in so arranging them, in so fixing his pennyworths of work. That he may attain his object—that manly independence without which no profession can be pleasant—it is not necessary that all the world should know the amount of return he make. It is only necessary that one person should know it;—and that one man will always know it. (219)

This understanding of professional work as something that could be effortlessly translated into exchange value did not address the complexity of intellectual labor, with its stored knowledge and developed expertise, nor did it address the awkward, indirect status of professional services within the mode of commodity production. As a theory of professional labor, in short, it was woefully inadequate. As a rhetorical strategy for Trollope's own career, however, one is tempted to say it was a triumph.

Self-Interested Labor as Authorial Strategy

The Three Clerks is not a novel of suspense. Trollope might simulate movement from time to time—making comments like, "What were the faults in [Harry's] character it must be the business of the tale to show" (5)—but, in fact, we always know where the novel is headed before we get there—even the above comment is hardly suspenseful, considering that the narrator says we must wait to learn Harry's faults right after he has finished describing them (namely, Harry's priggish sense of reserve). "It is not very pleasant," E. S.

Dallas wrote in his review of *The Three Clerks* for *The Times*, "to follow the windings of such a story, in which we see the end from the beginning" (108). In the only important criticism on the novel to date, Cathy Shuman makes an ingenious argument about this feature of the novel—what she calls its "static, fairytale quality" (92).[5] Realism and the exam, Shuman observes, both claim to read interiors, realism by "rel[ying] on a narrative surface encrusted with material objects that metonymically contain and define the penetrable depths within" and the exam by "reveal[ing] inner talent" ("Laborer and Hire" 88). Unlike both realism and the exam, Trollope's fiction refuses this illusion of depth, wherein things turn out to be other than what they first appear. Shuman argues that Trollope held empty labor or routine work in such high regard, because it is what it is without aspiring to be anything else. While Marx and others saw labor as vulnerable to alienation and abstraction, Trollope privileged labor, because it is, in another sense, inalienable—one must be present when one performs it—and immediately identifiable—one is either doing it or one is not. For Trollope, Shuman writes, "identity and value are metonymically rather than metaphorically related: a man may produce or possess value but he may not represent it" ("Laborer and Hire" 97). Shuman does not consider, however, the way this theory of value relates to Trollope's own heteronomous position in the literary marketplace. Placed within that context, Trollope's "theory" comes into view as an astute move within the literary game.

The Three Clerks was the first novel Trollope sold outright. With all five of his previous novels, he entered into half-profit share agreements with publishers. Novelists forced to enter into such contracts were "morbidly suspicious of how their profit share was calculated" (Sutherland 90). First shopping *The Three Clerks* at Longman's before selling it to Bentley's "out and out," as Trollope put it in his notes, he was told that Longman's would accept the novel only on half-profit terms. He wrote in his autobiography:

> When I went to Mr. Longman with my next novel *The Three Clerks* . . . I wished him to buy it from me at a price which he might think to be a fair value, and I argued with him that as soon as an author has put himself into a position which insures a sufficient sale of his works to give a profit, the publisher is not entitled to expect the half of such proceeds. . . . I thought that I had now reached that point, but Mr. Longman did not agree with me. And he endeavored to convince me that I might lose more than I gained, even though I should get more money elsewhere. 'It is for you,' said he, 'to think whether our names on your title-page are not worth more to you than the increased payment.' This seemed to me

> to savour of that high-flown doctrine of the contempt of money which I have never admired. I did think much of Messrs. Longman's name, but I liked it best at the bottom of a cheque. (108–9)

Mr. Longman asked Trollope to trade one form of capital for another, to exchange economic for cultural capital (the prestige of the imprint). In Trollope's view, the publisher attempted to invoke the artist's supposed disinterest, or distaste for money, so that he himself could laugh all the way to the bank.

"By depreciating his work through understatement, Trollope rhetorically enhances its value," Christina Crosby writes (295). Trollope's supposed devaluation of his work—repeatedly referring to his novels as mere commodities, for example—might have been strategic self-deprecation but it was also his way of refusing to be duped. Only the open market, in which even the most incommensurable objects—novel and cheque—could be rendered commensurable, ensured the fairness of a transaction. With the half-profits system by contrast, "the author was entirely dependent on the integrity of the publisher in rendering his accounts; it put an intolerable strain on the relationship" (Hamer 21). An arena of competing agents who do not pretend to be other than self-interested, the market provided a degree of transparency that, in turn, underwrote the value of professional labor. "Such a demand [of half-profits]," Trollope continued to sputter, "is monstrous as soon as the article produced is known to be a marketable commodity" (*Autobiography* 108).

Of course, by the rules Bourdieu outlines, Trollope might not have been seeing through the game of cultural capital so much as playing it badly. Perhaps he did not realize that a particularly impressive imprint might mean less profit now but more later. Certainly, in the short term, Trollope's choices, particularly his rhetorical presentation of those choices, hurt his reputation. The standard view is that his star fell precipitously after the publication of the *Autobiography*. If, as Paul Danahy writes in his study of Victorian autobiographies, "male authors represent themselves as autonomous and implicitly repress the social context of their labor" (3), Trollope's *Autobiography* in which he "unblushingly paraded sums, dates and details of contracts" must be the great exception (Sutherland 240).[6] Trollope famously focused on the material details of the context in which he wrote at the expense of the texts themselves. Margot Stafford writes of the *Autobiography*, "Trollope's bid to win respect for the profession only resulted in a loss of respect for himself" (7). "Of course all artistic work is done, to a great extent, mechanically," George Gissing admitted in *The Commonplace Book*, but Trollope "talked about it in a wrong and vulgar tone" (qtd. in Stafford 7).

But was Trollope any less read during this period in which critics looked askance at him for his seeming vulgarity? Is it possible, furthermore, that in the long run that very vulgarity was part of why he continued to survive—and, today, thrives—in the annals of criticism? If, as John Sutherland argued, artistic autonomy "was harder to come by and hold on to" for Trollope than for Dickens or George Eliot, then is it any surprise that given the choice between bought and unbought brains, Trollope chose to claim the image of the former (78)? By preemptively claiming it, Trollope could suggest that "true daring belongs to those who have the courage to defy the conformity of anti-conformity, even though they run the risk thereby of winning bourgeois applause," to quote Bourdieu on "bourgeois intellectuals" (*Rules of Art* 163).[7] Anticipating the highbrow reviewer's critique before he could make it, Trollope "turn[ed] his adversary's weapons against him by resolutely assuming the image instead of simply enduring it" (Bourdieu, *Rules of Art* 163). Choosing to represent himself in his *Autobiography*—and his hero in *The Three Clerks*—as a hack, but doing so in such a way that he appeared to have a *choice*, that it was something he ironically and self-reflexively embraced rather than simply endured, Trollope managed to escape being reduced to a hack by posterity. "Although he accepted the conditions that produced the hack novelist," Sutherland concluded, "Trollope was not a hack" (81).

What if we see Trollope's avowed and self-conscious predictability not as an "ostentatious *subversion* of realist conventions," as Shuman sees it, but as an ostentatious *submission* to those conventions (my emphasis, "Laborer and Hire" 89)? Slyly summing up one of *The Three Clerks*' central plots, Trollope's narrator says, "It need hardly be told in so many words to an habitual novel-reader that Charley did get his bride at last" (540–41). Yes, Trollope says here, I am playing by the rules, but I am no fool; I know what I'm doing. Winking at his readers, Trollope satisfied the average reader's expectations while also anticipating the elite reader's antipathy toward the formulaic. "React[ing] to the reaction of the intellectual critique which he is prepared to anticipate even before it has been formulated," Trollope wrote for a commercial market but attempted to arm himself against the critical consequences (Bourdieu, *Rules of Art* 163).

The Three Clerks ends with a scene in which Charley's mother-in-law reads aloud a review savagely critical of his latest novel, a review in fact playfully fabricated by Charley's wife Katie but one that apparently repeats criticisms now familiar to Charley in his lusterless career. The review reads: "No moral purpose can be served by the volumes before us. The hero acts wrongly throughout but nevertheless he is rewarded at last" (553). And it adds regarding Charley himself, that there is something about the novelist that "gives us the idea of a boy who is being rewarded for having duly learnt by rote his daily lesson" (552). This is, of course, an apt description of *The Three Clerks.* One unprincipled man overshoots himself and gets thrown back to the starting line, one overly principled man never goes anywhere, and a third man who is neither excessively ambitious nor unnecessarily self-denying behaves badly for awhile and, then, once he shows a little rote effort, gets what he was, in any event, most likely to get. The clergyman's son becomes a moderately successful professional and marries a clergyman's daughter. *The Three Clerks* is the story of a lack of distinct progress or maybe, more accurately, the story of predictable progress—a bildungsroman with an unheroic hero who develops only "the aptitude to be what [he] is" (Bourdieu, *Rules of Art* 11). One imagines that other unheroic hero Arthur Pendennis encountering these final pages of *The Three Clerks* in which Trollope preemptively reviewed the book he has just written. Skimming *The Three Clerks* as he struggles to finish his umpteenth book review that month, and having already jotted down the outline of his review, Pendennis reaches these last pages, curses Trollope, and starts from scratch—just the first in a long line of critics to be foiled by the position Trollope plotted for himself in the field of cultural production, brilliantly poised on the border between the canonical and the disposable.

CHAPTER FOUR

Deprofessionalized Critics in the Twenty-First Century

> Matters would be easy if we could merely say—naïvely—that the beauties of art must be subtracted from any politicization, or—knowingly—that the alleged autonomy of art disguises its dependence upon domination.
>
> —Jacques Rancière

> A key condition of any institutional politics . . . is that intellectuals do not denegate their own status as possessors of cultural capital; that they accept and struggle with the contradictions that this entails; and that their cultural politics should be openly and without embarrassment presented as their politics, not someone else's.
>
> —John Frow

When we study "the relation of the social structure to individual action," Talcott Parsons wrote of the professions in 1939, we find "that the dominant importance of the problem of self-interest has been exaggerated" (56). I have argued that by setting aside our critical fascination with the problem of self-interest—or with the hypocrisy of disinterest—we can see that the mid-nineteenth-century novel did not fashion professional identity primarily by flourishing the ideal of disinterestedness but rather by rhetorically negotiating their professionalizing protagonists' relationships to the market. By illuminating the labor involved in polishing the marriageable woman, *The Professor* assigns its professional the exchange value he needs at the same time as it grants him professional objectivity. William Crimsworth's disinterested—rather than lascivious—relations with his students result from the fact that he must view clearly the faults he renders invisible to future suitors. *David Copperfield* gives David professional disinterestedness not by denying his relationship to the market but by adopting one particular relationship to it rather than another—an industrial rather than speculative one. Born around the same time as the finance capitalist and also engaged in manipulating knowledge and symbols, the professional had to be distinguished from that suspicious figure, something Dickens accomplished by running his professional in the reliable time of the factory clock rather than the future-oriented time of speculation. Finally, in *The Three Clerks*, far from compromising professional integrity, the market ensures it. Refusing an ideology that mystifies the economics of art, Trollope's professional admits his self-interest and is rewarded with the kind of success that is, in fact, the best guarantee of good behavior. Trollope did not expect someone like Charley to behave well when placed in a disreputable office, but a good, well-run office like Weights and Measures called forth the qualities it both required and instilled. In this final chapter, I extend the insight discussed in the preceding chapter—that disinterest is a function more of circumstance than character—to an analysis of the debate over the state of the profession.

In the introductory chapter, I argued that Foucauldian criticism attained its dramatic influence in Victorian studies at least in part because it expressed—by displacing—the larger sociological reality of the profession. The relative helplessness and overdetermination of the Foucauldian subject rhymed with critics' experience of their own circumscribed agency. At the same time, with professional competition intensifying, producing a two-tiered system of stars and adjuncts, Foucault's account of a power-hungry expert class also made good common sense. Perhaps critics' eager mistrust of their nineteenth-century counterparts implied a self-indictment, as if outing the expert class absolved critics of their own troublingly redoubled will to power. Or perhaps, more simply, Foucault's description of experts planting in the populace what they then discover and cure—thereby generating their own careers in a sleight of hand—seemed accurate to critics working in a vocation that paid homage to the principle of disinterestedness but increasingly organized itself according to market logic. As with fantasy in general, there was nothing particularly rational about this dynamic wherein we experienced ourselves as at once powerless (in the face of the market) and megalomaniacal (in our pursuit of academic celebrity). Only yet inchoately grasping the dynamic downsizing the profession, how were we to know that both experiences of the professional self were related by-products of what Marc Bousquet ("Rhetoric of 'Job Market'" 212) calls "the structural transformation of the university"?

The structural transformation of higher education is a shift of power from faculty to administrators, who are reorganizing the conditions of academic labor. As a result, unless one's prolific publications catapult one to academic celebrity, one now faces "increased teaching loads, fewer funds for research, pressure to match research with the interests of corporate donors, higher standards for promotion and tenure, greater competition for fewer tenure lines, and, at some schools, the elimination of tenure altogether" (K. Newman 30). As the explicitness of this list suggests, the changes squeezing our profession are now in sharp focus. Today, most of us are clear that the problem lies not with careerist professionals who have forsaken—or never subscribed to—the ideal of disinterestedness but rather with the last three decades' steady *erosion* of professional autonomy and authority. Even as we loathed ourselves for our "expertness," that status was being taken away from us, and we were fast becoming "academic labor" or, in Gary Rhoades's intentionally oxymoronic phrase, "managed professionals."[1]

Mimicking industry's shift in the last thirty years from stable mass-scale production to flexible accumulation, universities and colleges are actively replacing salaried, tenure-line professors with waged adjunct labor bereft of benefits, security, or autonomy. The latest data show that 65 percent of college teaching is done by contingent faculty (AAUP). The number is undoubtedly higher in the humanities, whose required English, history, and other general studies classes generate plenty of work for non-tenured faculty and graduate students but whose faculty members, unlike their colleagues in science, business, or engineering colleges, are often unable to draw large amounts of funding to the colleges in which they work. Lacking directly apparent instrumental value, the humanities struggle to defend themselves as the market model consumes administrators' thinking. Situated at the point of greatest ideological tension is perhaps the English department and its faculty who "mak[e] a self-referential claim to authority which is not derived from the economic usefulness of their skills" (Martin 19). Not only is the scholarship of literature without obvious exchange value, but the notion of aesthetic value that historically justified the study of literature—and, thus, English departments—developed in direct opposition to exchange value. From roughly Kant forward, art became that which is *not* commodity, an opposition that generates the double discourse of value. This discourse, referred to throughout *Novel Professions*, distinguishes between "money, commerce, technology, industry, production and consumption, workers and consumers" and "culture, art, genius, creation and appreciation, artists and connoisseurs" (Smith 127). "In the first discourse," Smith writes, "events are explained in terms of calculation, preferences, costs, benefits, profits, prices, and utility. In the second, events are explained—or, rather (and this distinction/opposition is as crucial as any of the others), 'justified'—in terms of inspiration, discrimination, taste (good taste, bad taste, no taste), the test of time, intrinsic value and transcendent value" (127). The double discourse of value remained relatively intact, with some refinements and mutations, from the late eighteenth century until about the last quarter-century. It sought to keep its terms pure and separate, not only incommensurable but opposed: where economics is quantitative, aesthetics is qualitative; whereas commodities possess utility, art objects embody intrinsic value; and while one exchanges labor for wages, one participates in disinterested free play in art and literature. As it becomes clear that the profession needs to develop a strategy if it is to offer its practitioners a decent living, the question is: What do you do when the very terms with which you have traditionally defined yourself are in direct opposition to the only terms that now enjoy, well, purchase?

In the last five years, a handful of literary critics have tried to answer this question, and their answers typically take one of two positions. They either argue that we must revive the principle of disinterested service despite its marginality, hoping that whatever authority such a principle once enjoyed is not irrevocably lost, or they argue that we must unionize and fight the university in economic terms. The one strategy attempts to recuperate the discourse that asserts its incommensurability with the economic while the other appears to abandon that discourse by arguing for the value of literature not in the aesthetic language of transcendence but in the economic language of labor.

These two strategies reflect a long-standing tendency within literary criticism to oscillate between one discourse of value and the other, a pendulum effect that, as John Guillory's historical account of the double discourse of value in *Cultural Capital* makes clear, is built into criticism by the binary opposing aesthetics and political economy. Political economy and aesthetics's "separat[ion] at birth" dooms aesthetic criticism to an oscillation between exposing aesthetics's concealed exchange value and reasserting aesthetic disinterest (Guillory, *Cultural Capital* 303). (See chapter 1 for a more extended treatment of Guillory's account.) I sketch this oscillation's most recent manifestation here by juxtaposing a work paradigmatic of criticism in the 1990s, Martha Woodmansee's *The Author, Art, and the Market: Rereading the History of Aesthetics* (1994), to a recently published work in Victorian studies that is in some important respects its mirror other, Amanda Anderson's *The Powers of Distance: Cosmopolitanism and the Cultivation of Detachment* (2001). Drawing on Pierre Bourdieu's reflexive sociology, I then argue that once we widen the frame of analysis to include the sociological conditions in which these representative works were produced, we catch a glimpse of how and why the oscillation within criticism is reproducing itself within the debate over the profession.

In her influential study *The Author, Art, and the Market,* Martha Woodmansee argues that "the momentous shift from the instrumentalist theory of art to the modern theory of art as an autonomous object that is to be contemplated disinterestedly" occurred in reaction to the eighteenth-century development of a middle-class market for literature (32). The older instrumentalist theory of art which held that a work's purpose was to move its reader "was found to justify the wrong works," precisely because it justified those works the market rewarded. The aesthetic principle of disinterested autonomy, conversely, provided writers neglected by the market with a "set of concepts with which to address the predicament in which they found themselves—concepts by which (difficult, or 'fine') art's de facto loss of direct instrumentality could be recuperated as a (supreme) virtue" (32). For example, in her opening chapter "The Interests in Disinterestedness"—a title that, though he's never cited, seems taken from Bourdieu[2]—Woodmansee attributes Karl Philip Moritz's abandonment of his mentor's instrumental theory and his adoption of the principle of aesthetic autonomy to his mounting "financial worries" (29). He and the literary elite of which he formed a part found themselves to have been "betrayed by the profit motive and by the laws of supply and demand," she explains (28). "In the claim," continues Woodmansee, "that the 'true' work of art is the locus of intrinsic value—a perfectly self-sufficient totality that exists to be contemplated disinterestedly, for its own sake—Moritz makes a triumph of defeat and 'rescues' art from determination by the market" (32–33).

While much of Woodmansee's research—especially on the obscure Moritz who, it seems, articulated the logic of aesthetic autonomy a decade before Kant—is original, her point is not. In *Culture and Society* (1958), for example, Raymond Williams made the similar point that "there are some obvious elements of compensation" in the theory of aesthetic value (36). But unlike Woodmansee, Williams did not leave it at that. "Yet, undoubtedly," he continued, "this is to simplify the matter, for the response [of artists to postindustrial market forces] is not merely a professional one. It is also (and this has been of the greatest subsequent importance) an emphasis on the embodiment in art of certain human values, capacities, energies, which the development of society towards an industrial civilization was felt to be threatening or even destroying" (36). Woodmansee calls the principle of aesthetic value "convenient and very powerful," but it is its convenience for the professional egos involved that she explores and, other than as a vague reference to the principle's durability, what she means by "very powerful" is left unclear. As one reviewer complained, "her focus on the personal motivations of Moritz and Schiller seems to reduce the origin of modern aesthetics to a case of sour grapes on the part of individual writers" (Kaiser 104).[3]

Woodmansee's suspicion of the notion of disinterested aesthetic value pervades her text, evident even in the scare quotes in the sentence above: "Moritz 'rescues' art from determination by the market" (32–33). Was some kind of rescue *not* necessary? *Should* aesthetic value be determined solely, or even primarily, by exchange value? What separates her self-described "materialist" account from Raymond Williams's is its lack of dialectical reason. Exposing Kantian (or Moritzian) aesthetics' ideological side, Woodmansee seems to assume that she must then reject such aesthetics wholesale rather than seeing it as at once regressive *and* progressive.

In place of the high aesthetic tradition, Woodmansee champions an early-nineteenth-century form of reception theory that she finds in Francis Jeffrey, a follower of the associationist theory of aesthetics, which "privileg[ed] the recipient in a model of appreciation" (133). Jeffrey, she writes, was "convinced that aesthetic disagreement is not rationally resolvable, and [he was] entirely comfortable with diversity" (135). "Refreshingly current," as Woodmansee says, Jeffrey argued that there need not be a *standard* of taste. While this certainly reads more happily than any aesthetic that strives to adjudicate taste from above, it is, in the final analysis, indistinguishable from the market populism best loved by classical political economy wherein the consumer "cannot be wrong—except by consuming too little," as Woodmansee herself acknowledges (136). Rejecting an aesthetics of disinterest, Woodmansee reverts to an aesthetics uncritical of the market.

Such an aesthetic is the symmetrical counterpoint to Kantian aesthetics, then, but not necessarily in the way Woodmansee imagines. She conceives of Jeffrey's aesthetics as Kant's counterpoint because it privileged the spectator of art rather than the (difficult, self-sufficient) art itself, but as any reading of Kant or Schiller makes clear, the spectator was the privileged site of that version of aesthetics as well. The difference between the two versions, though, is that whereas Jeffrey assumed immediate (abstract) equality among spectators, Kant recognized that people are not all given equivalent access and potential as spectators—only those with full bellies, literally and figuratively, are capable of disinterested judgment. Although Jeffrey rightly eschewed snobbery, he might well be accused of a certain amount of bourgeois bad faith in his version of the spectator, a version that does not consider the inequality of the material conditions in which tastes develop. The aesthetic tradition may well have authorized a high culture in which only the leisured enjoyed aesthetic authority, but in its desire for a mode of perception liberated from economic necessity, the aesthetic tradition also acknowledged the material conditions inhibiting and distorting free judgment.

Amanda Anderson's *The Powers of Distance* attends to precisely the "distinctive virtues" of disinterest or "enabling detachment," in order to "enlarge and reframe current understandings of aesthetic and intellectual practice in nineteenth-century Britain" (5). (Anderson's use of the term "detachment," she tells us in her introduction, is meant to include the aesthetic notion of disinterestedness as well as scientific concepts such as critical reason.) Calling her book "polemical," she characterizes her approach as "go[ing] against the grain of much recent work in literary and cultural studies, which follows the critique of Enlightenment in its insistence that cultural ideals of rationality or critical distance are inevitably erected as the exclusive province of elite groups" (5). Anderson explores the ways in which various Victorians distinguished between forms of detachment. In "Disinterestedness as Vocation: Revisiting Matthew Arnold," for example, Anderson recovers "another line of thinking in Arnold's work" that emphasizes "the successful subjective enactment or embodiment of forms of universality, as distinguished from other moments where he seems to valorize impersonal or objective standards" (97). Rather than appealing to some fundamental, elitist standard of taste, then, as Anderson claims critics assume, Arnold focused on articulating "an ideal of temperament or character, whose key attributes bespeak a kind of value-laden value-neutrality: impartiality, tact, moderation, measure, balance, flexibility, detachment, objectivity, composure" (115).

Where Woodmansee did not acknowledge the critical force of disinterestedness, Anderson professes herself "devoted" to precisely this ideal (32). But if economic details appeared to hold too much weight in Woodmansee's analysis, they seem to carry no weight in Anderson's. Woodmansee simultaneously reduces aesthetics to the market (a lack of exchange value motivates the articulation of aesthetic value) and champions an aesthetic itself reducible to the market (consumer choice), but what marks Anderson's study is how little a mark the market leaves. Anderson cites Bourdieu in her introduction, quoting his statement that "the most effective reflection is one that consists in objectifying the subject of objectification" (30). However, she attempts to follow through on this advice not by analyzing the material conditions shaping her own perceptions but by remaining attentive to the ways in which the articulations of detachment she explicates in Arnold and others fall short. Yet, in turn, these figures do not fall short because of any disposition shaped by their material and social positions. Arnold, for example, is taken to task for his "inability to imagine reciprocal social relations as a site where one's principles might be enacted," but "the limits of his social and political vision" are presented as just that—limits of a vision, inadequacies of an individual. They are not understood as a consequence of Arnold's habitus or the logic of the field in which he moves. Anderson pays little attention to the economic and social conditions that predispose Arnold's thinking to expand in certain ways and contract in others.

When Anderson's approach throughout the book is held up to Bourdieu's actual methodology, it appears to fall into the very trap of idealist reflection Bourdieu criticizes. "One cannot avoid having to objectify the objectifying subject," Bourdieu writes; "It is by turning to study the historical conditions of his own production, rather than by some form or other of transcendental reflection, that the scientific subject can gain a theoretical control over his own structures and limitations" (*Rules of Art* xii). Consider Bourdieu's approach to "objectification" more generally. In *The Rules of Art*, for example, he submits the literary world of mid-nineteenth-century France to an intensive objectification by mapping each figure's position on the continuum of heteronomy (insertion in the market) and autonomy (distance from the market and economic necessity). By not analyzing the conditions in which her figures produce and are themselves produced, Anderson remains in the realm of transcendental reflection, unable to account for her figures' limitations or, for that matter, their achievements except as individual failures or feats of will and imagination.

Anderson wishes to reject what she calls the "all or nothing" form of criticism, arguing:

> Current critiques of detachment . . . [come to the] immediate and unwarranted assumption that any and all practices of cultivated distance claim a kind of pure or absolute objectivity for themselves. Countering with the view that no such objectivity exists, critics show themselves unable to imagine critical distance as a temporary vantage, an unstable achievement, or regulative ideal: it's all or nothing. (32)

Yet she inadvertently fosters just such a mode. First, by neglecting the material context in which such vantages and achievements become possible, Anderson fails to develop a discourse that can treat the (impure) material world and the (pure) ideal world in the same register, thereby implicitly and inadvertently reinforcing their dichotomous relationship. Secondly, the language that she does use, particularly such phrases as "temporary vantage" and "unstable achievement," suggests that disinterest is in itself pure but simply fleeting. Bourdieu's sociology of culture illuminates the logic by which "disinterest" is *simultaneously* self-interested and disinterested.

An engaged treatment of Bourdieu's work on aesthetic autonomy might have enabled both Woodmansee and Anderson to move beyond the either/or framework they establish wherein disinterest is either really disinterested or some masked form of self-interest. As I discussed in the introductory chapter, Bourdieu demonstrates in *Rules of Art* that the disinterested disposition is a function of the field—the habitus simultaneously selected and called into being. Viewing "disinterest" this way and not as evidence of certain individuals' extraordinary capacity for self-renunciation, we are more, rather than less, likely to believe in its authenticity.

Bourdieu's reframing of aesthetics constitutes a dialectical advance, taking us beyond the materialism/idealism opposition within which we have been stuck, shuttling between the two discourses. In fact, Bourdieu argues, this tendency to shuttle is built into the study of aesthetics:

> The science of art and literature is threatened by two opposite errors, which, being complementary, are particularly likely to occur since, in reacting diametrically against one of them, one necessarily falls into the other. The work of art is an object which exists as such only by virtue of the (collective) belief which knows and acknowledges it as a work of art. Consequently, in order to escape from the usual choice between celebratory effusions and the reductive analysis which, failing to take account of the fact of belief in the work of art and of the social conditions which produce that belief, destroys the work of art as such, a rigorous science of art must, *pace* both the unbelievers and the iconoclasts and also the believers, assert the possibility and necessity of understanding the work in its reality as a fetish; it has to take into account everything which helps to constitute the work as such, not least the discourses of direct or disguised celebration which are among the social conditions of production of the work of art *qua* object of belief. ("Field" 35)

While the "believers" uncritically assert the ideology of disinterest, the unbelievers disregard the collective belief in art's structural removal from the market and, in doing so, they distort their analyses while imagining that they dispel illusions. We must understand art "in its reality as a fetish," Bourdieu says—that is, as something that both is unaccounted for when accounted for by the deus ex machina of the "gift" or "genius" and yet also *is* a kind of deus ex machina because the traces of its production and the source of its origins have been obscured. Recognizing the effaced labor producing the "work of art *qua* object of belief" is to realize that art's transcendent position outside the market is itself a product of history. Historicizing the aesthetic ideal of autonomy is, then, not the same thing as reducing it to its compensatory and ideological functions, but nor is it to retrieve it from the ash heap in order to revalorize it. Historicizing the aesthetic ideal may lead to the realization, however, that it is changing now that the historical conditions that created it—the development of technologies of, and a market for, mass production—have themselves undergone substantial alteration.

Interestingly, the current debate over how to handle the profession's "crisis" reveals something about the ideal's transformation, if only symptomatically. To get at what it reveals, I return to Bourdieu's injunction to objectify the objectifying subjects by making room for the sociological conditions in which Woodmansee and Anderson produced their work. Why, that is, did an analysis of aesthetic autonomy that implicated it in the market logic it claimed to disavow make sense in the larger context of literary criticism in the 1990s? And why is a book rescuing aesthetic autonomy not from the market but from literary critics themselves necessary today?

The Author, Art, and the Market fit broadly within 1980s and 1990s post-structuralist work as part of the larger trend referred to in the introductory chapter as a hermeneutics of suspicion. It also fit with the development of cultural studies and the relatively new academic interest in popular culture. Helping to collapse the boundary between high and mass culture, Woodmansee's book suggests that the concepts of difficulty and self-sufficiency that authorize the privileging of high art are themselves in some sense unauthorized insofar as those that authored them did so for reasons other than the ones they gave. Anderson positions her study of the Victorians within the context of developments in literary criticism, and though she never mentions the larger sociological context of the English departments that house such criticism, her project might be viewed nonetheless as an implicit response to the increasing visibility of higher education's commercialization. It is no accident that as the humanities lose ground in the university, literary critics like Anderson find themselves wishing to reassert the possibility and integrity of disinterestedness. It is as if, after years of demystification and suspicion, critics find themselves in the ironic position of needing to reconstruct what they have just deconstructed. Indeed, exemplifying the oscillation of criticism within their own careers, some of the very critics who most effectively exposed the power dynamics underwriting apparently disinterested works during the "culture wars" of the 1980s and early 1990s are the ones now calling for a reassertion of disinterest. For example, Mary Poovey, whose demystification of "disinterest" in *Uneven Developments* I discussed in the introduction, has responded to the corporatization of the university by attempting to invigorate the discourse of aesthetic value.

In her essay "The Twenty-First-Century University and the Market: What Price Viability?" Poovey writes:

> We have to suspend the market model entirely in favor of an alternate system that defines value differently. The only way we can do this, in turn, is to identify, a priori, goods that are goods in themselves—that defy market evaluation because they are not quantifiable, thus not subject to commodification. In order to identify these goods—or more properly to assert they exist—I have to risk something that poststructuralism has taught me to abhor: I have to essentialize the 'human.' (6)

Acknowledging that her strategy requires her to unlearn the poststructuralism that shaped her scholarly work, Poovey articulates a rhetorical strategy that is, finally, the same one that English departments conventionally used *until* around 1970, when poststructuralism arrived: the assertion that aesthetics or, as Poovey puts its, "human creativity, is an end in itself, an autotelic, self-sufficient totality nonreferrable to market value. What is implied in this argument is that poststructuralism (and maybe cultural studies—all those literary critical modes governed largely or in part by a hermeneutics of suspicion) has inadvertently conspired with market ideology to destabilize the humanities. "I fear," Poovey writes, "that we have allowed our postmodern skepticism to neutralize the very criticism it initially fostered. By turning critique against the possibility of critique, I worry that we are helping the market render the very category of value meaningless" (7).[4] If we, at least in our "public" selves, get back to our old line—the aesthetic line that until a few years ago we excoriated as elitist, colonialist, and patriarchal but that we now see might have, as Anderson says, "distinctive virtues"—we might stem the tide of corporatization. "Ironically," Poovey writes, "the humanities' lack of economic potential may be the only asset capable of insulating us from market logic" (7). The very thing, then, that makes literary study so vulnerable—its inutility—might turn out to be its best defense.

Poovey is hardly alone. A growing number of literary critics worry that poststructuralism has destroyed a belief in the mission of literary studies at the very moment critics most need the power of their convictions. Director of the Association of Departments of English David Laurence worries that the hermeneutics of suspicion has led to "the erosion of conviction about the educational formation called literary studies and institutional formation called the English department" (17). David Bell complains that "Foucault's view of the literary as a field defined through exclusions and prohibitions . . . stoked the fires of suspicion toward literature" (488) and that a suspicious mode continues to prevail in literary studies: "The 'end of the age of high theory' . . . has not fundamentally changed the suspicion toward literature" (487). He writes:

> If we are to argue persuasively to undergraduates that a major in literature—or any study of literature, for that matter—is a worthwhile pursuit, then we need to explain why literature cannot simply be characterized as a field given over to power and its ruses. Unfortunately, the necessity for this explanation comes at a historical moment of suspicion when such an explanation is perhaps harder to provide than it has been before. (488)

Having argued that this is a "historical moment" and, thus, presumably, not something we can simply refuse when we think better of it, Bell nonetheless gives his essay the voluntaristic title "Moratorium on Suspicion?"—as if critics could agree to collectively shed a critical disposition that was two decades in the making now that it has become a professional liability.[5]

It is not hard to see why a rhetorical mobilization of "disinterest" is an appealing strategy at this point—it champions disinterest against profit as a vital human principle at a time when acting disinterestedly appears strange or self-defeating rather than noble. But there are at least three interrelated reasons why it is not a useful path to pursue.

First, from a certain perspective, it looks like an act of bad faith. Ruthlessly deconstructing the political and economic subtexts driving rhetoric elsewhere, the critic shies away from publicly disclosing the material reality, the struggle over class position and power within the university, that is the subtext of her own writing. While Poovey places her call for the rhetoric of aesthetic autonomy within this material context, she does not call for that context itself to be made publicly visible. Whereas the culture wars centered on the politics of race, sexuality, and gender, the crisis facing humanities departments now is clearly about class and economics (this economic crisis was already underway then, too, but was less visible). Asserting disinterest in this context is not an invocation of the "work of art *qua* object of belief" but a particular strategy for combating the market takeover of higher learning and for shoring up an eroding professorial class. It is the critic's subject position *as critic* (not as female, black, queer, and so on) that is at stake. In this case, rather than agitating for others or for her social group and, thus, *enacting* "disinterest" even as she exposes it as myth or alibi in texts, the critic must agitate for her own economic welfare. In this scenario, she cannot escape acknowledging explicitly that she is acting, in part, out of self-interest.

Recuperating the old model is, then, an unintentionally disingenuous strategy, but second, and more important, it will not do what these critics want it to. Though it may provide a rationale for what we do, a rationale will not defend English departments from retrenchment. As Michael Bérubé notes, "the market works by variables that have nothing to do with the profession's intellectual interests" (*Employment of English* 101). In other words, the hermeneutics of suspicion cannot be blamed for our alleged decline in enrollments—surely, students got as great a charge from interrogating as from revering literature—nor can it be blamed for administrators' penchant for phasing out tenure lines in the humanities. Administrators do not reduce English departments' tenure lines because they do not understand what humanities faculty do or how important they are—indeed, many administrators came straight out of humanities departments. They do it because they are under enormous budget pressures, and it is cheaper to hire adjuncts. Furthermore, administrators can hire adjuncts without experiencing much, if any, immediate loss of value. That is, it is certainly not the case that hiring literature adjuncts is "like staffing a hospital all with orderlies," as one pundit has claimed (*Businessweek*). Adjuncts are often just as qualified as, and sometimes more qualified than, their tenure-line counterparts. (Of course, over the long term, there is a very real loss in value—the loss in committee service, institutional loyalty and memory, and the like.) Under these circumstances, shared governance will continue to unravel and the gulf between faculty and administration will grow wider until it becomes unavoidably obvious that faculty can no longer count on the university as a whole to act as a profession but must defend their profession against a university increasingly dominated by the business model.

Lastly, even if a rationale could save us, it would not be disinterestedness. As commodity production shifts from mass-scale to elaborate and flexible niche marketing, aesthetic categories are necessarily destabilized. During the past century and a half or so, high art was never truly independent of the market, as its principle of autonomy proclaimed. Rather, as I discussed in the last chapter, it was independent of a particular market (the mass market) while it circulated upon what Bourdieu calls an antimimetic market, a field of restricted production in which producers' implicit audience is not the masses but other producers (see *The Field of Cultural Production*). High art relies conceptually upon the field of mass production by defining itself against it. As William Paulson explains, "The conjunction of mass literacy and the fully reproducible text made print the most advanced medium of marketed and marketable culture and thus made literature a leading early instance of an autonomous aesthetic field whose construction was both opposed to and facilitated by that impersonal and heteronomous cultural market" ("Market of Printed Goods" 403). With the structure of the impersonal, mass market fading, the categories "high" and "low" have been partially evacuated of meaning and force. This is part of a complex historical evolution that cannot be fully explored here.[6] For my purposes, it is enough to recognize that in this altered cultural and economic mode of production, the discourse of pure disinterest collapses into contradiction. We can capitalize on our "lack of economic potential" as our greatest "asset," Poovey writes, contradictorily adopting market vocabulary to champion market transcendence. Of course, Poovey knows very well what she's doing—this is the irony she alludes to—but precisely in knowing what she is doing, she reminds us that the double discourse of value no longer pretends to keep its terms separate and pure. It never *could* keep them separate and pure, but this fact was not acknowledged or, if so, only fleetingly and relatively incoherently. Such "innocence" was embodied in the two discourses' various practitioners. That what used to be an embodied strategy has become a self-conscious one indicates that the double discourse of value no longer functions the way it used to. Perhaps nothing underscores this change more than the recent media attention given Jonathan Franzen's reluctance to have Oprah Winfrey's Book Club stamped on his novel. Of the incident, David Kirkpatrick wrote in the *New York Times*, "After disparaging Oprah Winfrey's literary taste . . . [Franzen] was full of abashed apologies." This shows, Kirkpatrick continues, "that if there was ever a time in the book business when authors wrote to impress critics and their peers without regard to book sales, getting caught in that posture is now almost embarrassing."

In an analysis of the contemporary literary prize scene which beautifully illustrates the fact that the once-repressed logic opposing economic and aesthetic value has become conscious, fundamentally altering the "game," James English writes that "without disappearing, the modern discourse of autonomy has become a tactical fiction, or at least an imperfectly sincere one" (124). Paulson, too, sees this new self-consciousness as reflective of a fundamental reorganization of cultural and economic logic: "It hardly seems possible anymore to base a theory and defense of intellectual autonomy on the institutions and practices of print, at least not without recognizing that such a theory and defense are calculated exercises in the strategic maintenance of residual formations" ("Market of Printed Goods" 405). And, indeed, calculation and strategy are everywhere apparent in the tone of Poovey's essay. "In order to identify these goods [in themselves]—or more properly to assert they exist," Poovey begins one sentence, highlighting her argument's strategic essentialism by switching from a register of naive empirical belief to an ironic register that underlines its rhetorical status. Simultaneously full-throated and self-ironizing, Poovey juggles agency as if it were a hot potato, embracing a position and signaling her distance from it in the same moment. "I have to risk something that poststructuralism has taught me to abhor," she writes:

"I have to"—I am forced against my will or perhaps better judgment to—"risk something"—take a position I'm not sure I can defend.

Poovey's essay represents a new twist in literary criticism's oscillation between exposing the exchange value concealed in aesthetic value and asserting the disinterest of aesthetic value. She side-steps what might be called the double bind of the double discourse, that bind whereby embracing the one discourse inexorably means disavowing the other. Instead, she signals some solidarity with *both* discourses by managing a tone at once sincere and ironic. Such an argument strangely echoes Bourdieu's own, as he describes the literary and artistic field as a field that operates in bad faith but that does so in all sincerity. (More specifically, in "The Production of Belief," Bourdieu calls the literary and artistic field a "bad faith economy" while elsewhere, particularly in *Rules of Art*, insisting on the sincerity of those who maneuver within it—a contradiction that yields a dialectical truth.) Of course, the difference is that Bourdieu aims to explain the (receding) logic of symbolic capital while Poovey wishes to reanimate it, placing herself not among the sociologists of culture but its defenders. Thus, what Bourdieu's sociology seeks to disclose is precisely what Poovey's strategy is necessarily predisposed to repress: labor. For Poovey, the emphasis falls on the "goods in themselves"—the artifacts that, to recall Smith's distinction, can be justified in terms of creativity and uniqueness but cannot be explained or quantified as products of labor. For Bourdieu, the sociology of culture entails unearthing the enormous rhetorical, institutional, and individual labor that produces the "work of art" both as a material or linguistic object and as an "object of belief" and which, in order to succeed, was repressed *as labor*. Tracing the construction of the aesthetic discourse of disinterestedness, *Rules of Art* shows that the discourse is hardly universal or essential but rather developed to do necessary cultural work—specifically, the work of autonomization.

If the discourse of disinterest authorized the historical autonomization of literary study, then it makes sense that critics would come to see poststructural, politically informed work as complicit with the devaluation of the profession. But scrambling to reverse course by defending aesthetic value will only perpetuate what Jeffrey J. Williams calls "the ideological gap, between the imaginary projection of motivation and goals in the humanities (fun, spiritual improvement) and the actual conditions of employment in universities" ("Life of the Mind" 209). Instead of reversing course, what if we were to see the rise of political criticism not as an inadvertent accomplice in the marginalization of literature but as a useful, if unrecognized, response to it? Guillory has made a less hopeful version of this argument in a widely read piece on the profession in the *ADE Bulletin*. Guillory suggests that rather than having exacerbated the current crisis, the hermeneutics of suspicion was an ill-fated, only half-conscious attempt to forestall it. Sensing their obsolescence, literary critics responded by increasing their volume, in both senses—by producing more words and by being louder (in other words, more politically strident and attention-seeking). Hyperprofessionalized, hyperpoliticized graduate students, on Guillory's reading of this behavior, act this out in exaggerated fashion, embodying the bid of an "increasingly irrelevant" discipline for political and professional power (4). "What I call preprofessionalism is nothing other than the realm in which the profession's fantasies, both professional and political, are acted out," he writes ("Preprofessionalism" 6).[7] As I discussed in the introduction, Guillory views this political criticism as almost grandiosely deluded in its sense of its own potential impact. Instead, economic forces out of our control doom us to deprofessionalization.[8]

I want to end *Novel Professions* by asking whether a less defeatist narrative than Guillory's might be constructed, one in which his own work stands as evidence of what the last twenty years has made possible. Perhaps he articulates so clearly what the rest of us express as garbled symptom precisely because the profession *has* become increasingly political. Is it such a great leap, after all, from doing work in the name of a number of constituencies—feminist, queer, minority, postcolonial, and the like—to doing work in the name of our own constituency—the professional class? This heightened self-reflexivity—the objectification of the self, in the positive Marxist sense—might be possible now only because of feminist awareness of situated epistemologies, Foucauldian suspicion of liberal individualism, and, for that matter, Bourdieuian sociology, which has uncovered the material production of "disinterest." However paradoxical at first glance, political criticism's exposure of the material underpinnings of the liberal or aesthetic ideology of autonomy may be seen as precisely the precondition for our present recognition that our (relative) autonomy is endangered as well as the precondition for our willingness to adopt a political disposition earlier generations of gentlemen scholars were trained to abhor.

At the very least, the existence of these modes of critical thought (feminist, Foucauldian, queer, postcolonial, Bourdieuian, and so on) signals the improbability of recovering the ideal of disinterestedness as an unconscious component of our habitus.[9] And this may be a good thing, if it leads us to abandon an ideal that encourages us to work, if not for free, then at a substantial discount. (Andrew Ross uses the phrase "cultural discount" to refer to the principle whereby certain kinds of "workers accept nonmonetary rewards—such as the gratification of producing art [or of teaching literature]—as compensation for their work, thereby discounting the cash price of their labor" ["Mental Labor Problem" 6]). Whereas Guillory views political criticism as essentially superstructural—"The politicization of the humanities is an effect of the latter's marginalization and not the other way around," he writes ("Literary Critics" 115)—the case might be made that political criticism responds in turn by making possible new resistance to the managerial marginalization of literary studies.[10] The self-reflexivity it engenders might motivate us to advocate "openly and without embarrassment," as John Frow writes, for ourselves as professionals with the right to organize our own labor.

Rather than a highly sophisticated blind alley, then, the last two decades' deconstruction of disinterest might have cleared the way for a dialectical advance. At his best, for example, Foucault did not condemn experts but rather shifted the epistemological terrain they inhabit by calling upon us to "abandon the opposition between what is 'interested' and what is 'disinterested'" (*Discipline and Punish* 28). Bourdieu—not to mention the Victorian novel itself—has already begun this post-Kantian work. Identifying the self-interest central to the historical production of "disinterest," Bourdieu identifies the conditions in which disinterest becomes possible. Whereas others have also spotlighted the material context of disinterest, they have tended to assume that such illumination necessarily damns disinterestedness, exposing the naked emperor. Instead of continuing to exaggerate the problem of disinterestedness, whether by damning its hypocrisy or defending its nobility, critics need to focus on work autonomy, because autonomy is simultaneously a self-interested luxury and the material condition for genuine service. In our English departments, in public forums, and at the bargaining table, we need to fight to preserve intellectual autonomy by fighting to preserve the tenure-line appointments that make it possible, because, as Bourdieu warns, "durable virtues cannot be established on a pure decision of conscience. If disinterestedness is sociologically possible, it can be so only through the encounter between habitus predisposed to disinterestedness and the universes in which disinterestedness is rewarded" (*Practical Reason* 88).

Notes

Notes to Introduction

1. For an insightful discussion of the way the word "smart" operates in academic circles, see Jeffrey J. Williams. As Bourdieu writes, "Nothing classifies somebody more than the way he or she classifies" ("Social Space" 132).

2. See Dweck and Nicholls. See also Malcolm Gladwell's essay "The Talent Myth" in which he discusses Dweck's work.

3. See Wooldridge for a fascinating history of the IQ test. Wooldridge is uncritically liberal, however; for more critical accounts, see Gould, Kamin, and Gillian Sutherland. See Lemann for a discussion of the IQ test in America.

4. This tendency to turn "doing" into "being" annoys *Punch* as early as 1853 when the editors write, "We are continually hearing of some individual or other who is remarkable for what is called an 'Enlarged Benevolence.' We wish MR. DONOVAN would explain to us the meaning of this phrase, for though we sometimes hear of an enlargement of the heart, or of a newspaper having been permanently enlarged, we are puzzled to understand how there can be an enlargement of an individual's benevolence." "A Phrenological Puzzle."

5. "The challenge posed to class analysis by the group in question," Guillory has written, "is precisely that of a class in which the cultural constituent appears to be definitive, and in which its mode of cultural or 'knowledge' production is *uniquely* related to the system of production" ("Literary Critics as Intellectuals" 124).

6. Because, as Harold Perkin wrote, "it was chiefly in the civil servants . . . that the professional ideal began to diverge from the entrepreneurial," I focus in *Novel Professions* on the civil service rather than the Oxbridge examinations, but the former were modeled upon the latter (*Rise of Professional Society* 428).

7. "To a much greater degree than is usually credited," Hack writes, "authors . . . accept market exchange as one—if not the only—source of income that does not compromise one's independence, and even to highlight their participation in the marketplace" ("Literary Paupers" 693).

8. Adams is referring specifically to the way Foucauldian critics have written about domesticity in Victorian culture. "Many recent accounts of Victorian domesticity," he writes in his extremely useful 2001 review of work in the nineteenth century, "have restaged versions of what one might call Foucauldian melodrama: the familiar story of the many-headed Hydra of 'surveillance' violating the sanctity of domestic privacy" ("Recent Studies in the Nineteenth Century" 858–59).

9. In *The History of Sexuality*, Foucault writes, "The question I would like to pose is not, Why are we repressed? but rather, Why do we say, with so much passion and so much resentment against our most recent past, against our present, and against ourselves, that we are repressed?" (8–9).

10. See Guillory's "Preprofessionalism" and also Lambert on Guillory's essay.

11. In his critique of this narrative of decline, Bruce Robbins contrasts this perception of professionalization to "vocation": "Vocation demands public-ness and progress [while] professionalization means privacy and regress," he writes (*Secular Vocations* 121). For a fascinating analysis of how the "common tale of a Fall into Professionalism" haunts numerous disciplines in addition to literature, see Robbins's "Less Disciplinary Than Thou" (11).

12. In *Literary Culture in a World Transformed*, William Paulson makes a similar (and similarly bleak) argument. "Literature's overt value as cultural capital for the upper-middle class," he writes, "has been declining for generations, to the point that it is futile either to try to prop up its archaic function as the font of refined, genteel discourse or to claim that one is striking a blow for democratic culture by debunking it" (14).

13. For examples in which Guillory is explicitly cited as an influence in the authors' thinking, see David Laurence's "The Latest Forecast," Mary Poovey's "Beyond the Literary Critical Impasse," and George Levine's "Two Nations."

14. As John McGowan explains, the assault on professorial autonomy is "connected with the contemporary economy's maximizing of productivity through use of a modified piecework system. Workers are only hired for the specific time and the specific tasks for which they are needed, and are not carried by the employer during slack times" (43).

15. The American Association of Higher Education is arguably one of the major players in the move to abolish tenure. Their "New Pathways" series is devoted to developing new ways to organize higher education, and, repeatedly, articles in this series recommend the abolishment of tenure. "The view espoused in this paper is that tenure may have made some sense in the 1920s, or in the 1960s," begins one article, "but may not make sense as the dominant employment relationship in the 1990s or the decade beyond" (Breneman 2).

16. Since 1975, the number of non-tenure-track faculty has increased by 88 percent (Harris 27). At my own university, something like 70 percent of the English department's student-credit hours are taught by non-tenure-line faculty. Not only are literature students taught by "casual labor" but much of our departmental service is performed by non-tenure-line faculty. For example, our assistant chair is not tenure-line.

17. Tellingly, the implications of the very phrase "job market" have changed. Once, applying the phrase to the annual shuffle between departments and job seekers seemed to operate as mere analogy. After all, literary critics chose their profession in part to escape the market logic that presides over other employment sectors. In a second phase, the "market" is invoked ruefully and ironically—"look we're just like everybody else after all, a big cut-throat game." Now, little trace of irony remains as the phrase "job market" saturates our conversations, no longer as trope but as apparent reality. Marc Bousquet has argued persuasively, however, that the rhetoric of the "market" does not describe but rather obscures our current dilemma ("Rhetoric of 'Job Market,'" "Waste Product"). The sense that large market forces are behind the job crisis leaves us less likely to resist the structural transformation of higher education, and the focus on the job market "diverts attention from the real problems of 'demand' (the willingness of administration to utilize nonde-

greed flexible labor instead of degreed persons in jobs)" ("Rhetoric of 'Job Market'" 215).

18. For an early articulation of the same logic by an Americanist, see Seltzer, who wrote in *Henry James and the Art of Power*, "Modern power arrangements of discipline and normalization aspire to a 'double discourse' of disavowal and reinscription. From this point of view, the assertion of literary autonomy or subversiveness appears not as an escape from power but rather as part of that power's deployment" (174).

19. Poovey's suspicion extends even to points incidental to her argument. She describes book reviewing, for example, as if professionals—notoriously unlikely to identify *as* a class because of professionalism's emphasis on individual merit—were conspiring to guarantee one another's value. Mentioning one review of *David Copperfield* in *Fraser's Magazine* (a journal without any obvious stake in the novel's success), she places "review" in scare quotes and claims, "like many other mid-nineteenth-century 'reviews,' this piece functions as an advertisement for the novel, but because it is presented as a critical evaluation, it generates the effect of describing the value it actually helped create" (108). Of course, there is some truth to this, and one could imagine an argument that illustrates all the diverse kinds of labor, some invisible, that go into the production of "value." Poovey's comment, however, reflects a thoroughgoing cynicism about the nature of professional practices.

20. With his usual clarity on the topic, Robbins makes the point that the "logic of self-constitution by means of exclusion cannot be taken for granted. It is true, of course, that credentials are only meaningful if someone else does not possess them. Yet there is a very long step from this truth to the more questionable notion that the unequal possession of credentials is necessarily unjust. There is another long step to the more dubious assumption that unequal credentialing is the central principle of injustice in our unjust society" (*Secular Vocations* 200).

21. In an essay on aesthetics and modernity, Harpham drew up a list of "norms and notions" central to aesthetics that chimes remarkably well with professionalism: "the privilege of disinterested assessment; the autonomy of the artifact from historical, social, or economic forces; the uncoerced liberty of the judging subject; the universability of subjective responses; the human capacity to imagine and create objects" ("Aesthetics and the Fundamentals of Modernity" 124).

22. For an example of a work written in the heyday of suspicion but which brilliantly kept art's double position front and center, see Psomiades.

23. I should note that in her recent essay "Beyond the Current Impasse in Literary Studies" Poovey admits that she has been one of those critics who, among other things, "assum[ed] that neither literary texts nor other kinds of cultural artifacts belong to separate or autonomous domains" (368). As indicated here and in a handful of other places, Poovey might agree with some of the criticisms I forward here.

24. For an excellent explanation of why Bourdieu has been read this way, see Moi. Moi argues that critics accustomed to the poststructural seesaw of oppositions—"subject or object, activity or passivity, voluntarism or determinism" (503)—find it difficult to do what Bourdieu requires, which is to "grasp and hold both sides of the formulation 'to make something of what the world makes of us'—our freedom as well as the necessity that constrains it" (503). As a result, poststructural critics tend to reduce Bourdieu's work to mere determinism, absorbing it as "just another poststructuralist 'theory'" (506).

25. James Chandler has recently suggested that literary critics need to "work toward a

better understanding of how the scheme of disciplines might be said to compose a system" (359). Pointing to Bourdieu's work as a resource for such a project, Chandler continues, "my sense is that the totality of the disciplines at any given time should be articulated not as a set of territories, or even as a set of parallel functions, or box of tools, but as a network of relatively autonomous practices in asymmetrical relation to each other" (360).

26. A more detailed exploration of the differences between the French and English nineteenth centuries would help clarify the limitations of Bourdieu's project for Victorianists, but here I am primarily concerned to use him to inspire a new line of inquiry. In a fascinating discussion of Victorian poetry and modernity, Ivan Kreilkamp asks a question relevant to my own project on the novel. Invoking the figure in *Rules of Art* second only to Flaubert, Baudelaire, he asks, "Why do we have no English Charles Baudelaire, no mid-nineteenth-century poet whose work participates, explicitly and consciously, in the early theorization of modernity occurring at the time in France and Germany and America? Is it possible that this lack is at least in part a by-product of the questions we ask of Victorian poetry?" (605). I suggest that our sacrifice of the Victorian professional has been a major factor prohibiting an analysis of the Victorian novel in relationship to aesthetic modernity.

27. Rather, he continues, "it is by increasing [intellectuals'] autonomy (and, thereby, among other things, their freedom to criticize the prevailing powers) that intellectuals can increase the effectiveness of political action whose ends and means have their origin in the specific logic of the fields of cultural production" (340).

28. There is perhaps a little self-loathing to Jameson's sacrifice of the pompous-humble intellectual, a bizarre moment in which Jameson and Winston Churchill converge in Churchhill's remark that "the intelligentsia are the glittering scum on the deep river of production" (qtd. in Lubenow 8).

29. As David F. Noble explains, "With the commoditization of instruction, teachers as labor are drawn into a production process designed for the efficient creation of instructional commodities, and hence become subject to all the pressures that have befallen production workers in other industries undergoing rapid technological transformation from above" (*Steal This University* 39). Long before the University of Phoenix was even an idea much less a reality, Marx said, "A schoolmaster is a productive labourer, when, in addition to belabouring the heads of his scholars, he works like a horse to enrich the school proprietors. That the latter has laid out his capital in a teaching factory, instead of a sausage factory, does not alter the relation" (*Capital* 1: 16,509).

30. Here, and throughout *Novel Professions,* I tend to use Marxist vocabulary and concepts, but this image of creative labor that returns to its producer might just as easily be put in psychoanalytic terms as work that augments and integrates the ego rather than diminishes it. In D. W. Winnicott's terms, it is the difference between "creative apperception" and "compliance."

31. Paul Delany also criticizes "the predominant influence of Foucault" (5). "England and France," he writes, "have such fundamental differences as to make it implausible that the Foucauldian model would have equal explanatory power on both sides of the Channel" (5–6).

32. As Mintz discussed at much greater length, "George Eliot examines both how far the conditions of the age made it possible for the impulse toward self-aggrandizing ambition and the impulse toward selfless contribution to society to be united in a single life,

and, in addition, how that union is supported by secularized versions of older Protestant ideas about a man's calling in the world" (2).

33. This self-loathing is not the same as that identified by Stanley Fish in his notorious 1994 essay "The Unbearable Ugliness of Volvos." The implicit self-glorification Fish identifies in academic martyrdom has largely evaporated, I would argue, now that we have become increasingly reliant upon exploiting adjunct labor.

Notes to Chapter One

1. For key examples of the first argument, see Larson, Heyck, and Wiener. For what is perhaps *the* key example of the second, see Poovey's "The Man-of-Letters Hero."

2. The apparently contradictory position of the professional between labor and capital has been widely acknowledged since Barbara and John Ehrenreich's seminal essay "The Professional-Managerial Class" in which they examined the professional's ambivalent relationship to the capitalist interests he or she serves. I take the title of this chapter from *Between Labor and Capital*, a 1979 essay collection focused on the Ehrenreichs' argument. For an important reworking of their premise, see Robbins's "The Village of the Liberal-Managerial Class."

3. One reason Brontë felt *The Professor* possessed more "substance" than *Jane Eyre* might have been that she perceived the former male-narrated novel to be primarily about work and only secondarily about romance while she saw the later novel to reverse these priorities. In other words, she may have been betraying her participation in her culture's common sense that work is serious, substantive, and intrinsically masculine while romance is silly, ephemeral, and feminine. Nonetheless, one by-product of this novel's production of a male professional is, as I will argue later, a rather rigorous refusal of the logic that assigns women to the play or non-work side of the labor/play divide.

4. For a more developed account than Guillory's of the origins of aesthetic disinterestedness in eighteenth-century philosophy, see Stolnitz. For an excellent and fascinating discussion that places the origins of aesthetics in relationship to the rise of bourgeois state structures, see Lloyd. "My fundamental argument," wrote Lloyd, "is that the discourse on the aesthetic supplies theoretical resolution to the antinomies of bourgeois politics, resolutions which inform not only subsequent ideological discourse but also its material institutions" (109).

5. For a discussion of Burke's definitions, see Poovey's "Aesthetics and Political Economy in the Eighteenth Century."

6. See Armstrong and Tennenhouse for a discussion of Marx's inability to account for intellectual labor.

7. The initial framing of the novel might be understood in this context not as a false start, as has often been argued, but as a reproduction of this structure. Beginning as a letter to an old school friend, the novel abandons this device as if the epistolary form were too tied to an older, obsolete economy of patronage. William tells us that the "time . . . which I intended to employ for his [friend's] benefit, I shall now dedicate to that of the public at large" (47). But the modern mass-marketed commodity turns out to be an unacceptable form as well. While Crimsworth dedicates his story to the "public at large," he quickly rules out a large public by adding: "My narrative is not exciting, and above all, not

marvelous [*sic*]; but it may interest some individuals, who, having toiled in the same vocation as myself, will find in my experience frequent reflections of their own" (47). The story is dedicated not to an undifferentiated, impersonal market, but to "individuals" on the same career path. The book's relationship to the market is much like the modern professional's: both circulated on the market, they nonetheless attempt to protect themselves from its universalizing and homogenizing effects.

8. Making a similar point, the Newcastle Commission reported in 1861, "Trained teachers do not dislike their work; there is no reason why they should; it is honourable, intellectual, and benevolent; but society has not yet learned how to value them. This they feel with all the sensitiveness that belongs to educated and professional men" (qtd. in Sturt 159).

9. A great deal of work has explored phrenology in its political and scientific contexts. As well as Cooter, see Shapin, Richards, Harrington, and Clarke and Jacyna. For discussions of Brontë and phrenology, see Shuttleworth and Dames ("The Clinical Novel"). For a discussion of professionalization and phrenology, see my "The Case of *The Zooist*."

10. Critics have seen Crimsworth as a class hybrid but nobody has noticed that he is in fact a protoprofessional. Terry Eagleton has argued that the novel enacts "a marriage of identifiably bourgeois values with the values of the gentry or aristocracy" but his marriage metaphor obscures the hard work the novel performs as it rewrites the aesthetic and aristocratic versions of independence into a middle-class notion of professional autonomy (54).

11. If, as Dierdre D'Albertis has argued, "the principles of duty and self-denial intrinsic to professional identity on the one hand, and to gender classification on the other, undercut one another," then it might be worth hypothesizing that Brontë's refusal of the tie between disinterest and femininity is a strategy to make room for a representation of herself as a disinterested *professional* (4).

12. The tension between mental work and mental property that exists in the novel reflects a tension that existed within phrenology itself. Phrenology was popularly understood as a form of material determinism—one's skull defined and delimited you—but, in fact, the phrenological movement at mid-century thought that one might exercise and improve one's abilities. But the popular understanding was not simply a mistake but rather an acknowledgment that by stressing the structure of seemingly unchangeable matter, phrenology appeared to reduce one to one's material property even as it argued for one's self-improvement through labor.

13. In a novel that is anything but playful, one that in fact redefines play as labor, economic metaphors repeatedly miss their mark. Toward the end of the novel, Crimsworth says to Frances after having agreed to a request of hers, "'Now as a reward for such ready consent, give me a voluntary kiss.'" "She brought her lips into very shy and gentle contact with my forehead," the novel continues; "I took the small gift as a loan, and repaid it promptly, and with generous interest" (251). We are to feel that Crimsworth and Frances's relationship is governed by a logic so completely different from economics that economic terms are humorous when invoked between them. I would venture to say that for most readers this passage does not achieve its desired effect. It is not so much that the dialogue is cloying, though it is that, but that transforming a gift into a loan does not seem so playful when performed by a protagonist who has consistently taken things that should be outside the logic of exchange and placed them within the tit-for-tat of commerce.

14. Heather Glen wrote in her 1989 introduction to the novel, "Recent critics . . . often trac[e] the novel's 'flaws' to the fact that it is the only one of Charlotte Brontë's published works to adopt the point of view of the male narrator" (7). Glen herself argued that the novel is a satire of Victorian masculinity. While an ingenious way of accounting for the discomfort the novel provokes, this argument is not very persuasive, because, as Alan Rauch has more recently explained, "The Crimsworth family embodies an ideal that would have suited Brontë and many of her readers" (159). For his part, Rauch does not then try to account for readers' dissatisfaction with the text, merely suggesting that "*The Professor* bears the mark of a first effort if only because it is optimistic and uncomplicated in a way that Brontë's later novels are not" (159). Optimistic, perhaps, but the novel is certainly not uncomplicated. My argument suggests, in fact, that the novel's failure is in part due to its quite complicated structure, one in which the two sides—labor and capital—collapse in on one another.

Notes to Chapter Two

1. Miller and Poovey "continue to set the terms for discussions of the interpellative effects of Dickens's fictions," Rachel Ablow writes (40). Gareth Cordery's 1998 essay "Foucault, Dickens, and David Copperfield" might be a case in point. "David simply exchanges one form of social discipline that is openly repressive and corporeal for another that is covert and internal," Cordery writes, going on to show how Miller's argument can account for even those parts of the novel Miller does not address (71).

2. Similarly, Amanda Anderson writes about *Little Dorrit*, "The suspicious approach cannot do justice to Dickens, who . . . not only critically acknowledges the unholy alliance between British nationalism and global capitalism, but conveys a highly complicated understanding of the gains and losses of detachment cultivated in the service of systemic critique" (66).

3. "Everything with him went as by clockwork," Dickens's housekeeper and sister-in-law Georgina Hogarth recalled of Dickens (qtd. in Ackroyd 561). Echoing Copperfield's comment regarding his own timely "discharge" of literary duties, one of Dickens's sons claimed of his father, "no city clerk was ever more methodical or orderly than he: no humdrum, monotonous, conventional task could ever have been discharged with more punctuality or more business-like regularity, than he gave to the work of his imagination and fancy" (qtd. in Ackroyd 561).

4. For discussions of time in *Dombey and Son*, see Greenstein and Baumgarten. For a fascinating survey of illustrations of watches and clocks in Victorian literature, with special consideration of those in Dickens's novels, see Dillon.

5. "They mutilate the labourer into a fragment of a man," Marx wrote; "they estrange from him the intellectual potentialities of the labour-process in the same proportion as science is incorporated in it as an independent power" (*Capital* 1: 604).

6. In addition to Roach, see R. J. Montgomery's *Examinations: An Account of Their Evolution as Administrative Devices in England*. Montgomery wrote, "1850 marked the beginning of a decade in which examinations became really popular. Competitive examination, in particular, was held up as a panacea for many educational or social ills. So many systems were started in this period that it appears as a sort of spring or source, the sub-

stance of which comes rolling down in the years in the form of one famous public examination system after another" (41).

7. This "triumph" was so complete that J. G. Fitch could argue in a speech to the Social Science Association as early as 1858: "No phenomena in the educational horizon at all approach in importance the rapid extension of a system of examination hitherto almost exclusively confined to the students in the Universities—first to candidates for appointments in the military, naval, and civil service of the Crown; then, to alumni of mechanics' institutions, by the Society of Arts; then, to the boys of middle-class schools, by the College of Preceptors, and by the Universities; and, lastly, to the children of National British and other elementary schools, in the form of prize and certificate schemes" (qtd. in Roach 73).

8. For an excellent article on the role of the examination in *Our Mutual Friend*, see Shuman ("Invigilating"). Like me, Shuman is interested in how the professional uses the examination to shore up his authority and carefully negotiate a relationship to the market; but, where I primarily address the problematic temporality of the examination, Shuman's emphasis lies with the specifically gendered ways Dickens puts the exam to use.

9. See chapter 3 for a more in-depth discussion of this issue of distinguishing, as one article put it, "the quality of the mind [from] the quantity of the stores with which it is furnished" (Morison 538). Numerous articles on Civil Service and university examinations in journals such as *Chambers Journal*, *Fortnightly Review*, *Cornhill Magazine*, and *Fraser's Magazine* discussed the "problem of cramming," cramming being defined by one article as "the accumulation of undigested facts and second-hand theories to be reproduced on paper" (Sayce 838).

10. For a different reading of Mr. Dick's copying, see Welsh, "Writing and Copying in the Age of Steam." Welsh argued that at a time when mechanical reproduction was rapidly dissolving the difference between the original and the copy, the copy, in essence, rose in value. *David Copperfield* participates, then, in the "relatively straightforward Victorian celebration of writing and copying" (45). While this is an ingenious argument, it overlooks the fact that copying is distinctly associated in the novel with those who are *limited* in power, incapable of more imaginative pursuits.

11. We know a character in this novel by the way she or he treats time. Though he is very industrious, Traddles is, we realize, somehow fundamentally inadequate when the adult David see Traddles "looking at his plain old silver watch" and notes that it is "the very watch he once took a wheel out of, at school, to make a water-mill" (598). On the one hand, Traddles *wears* a watch, a good sign, but, on the other hand, he puts it to inappropriate uses, a telltale sign that something is wrong. Indeed, what ends up being wrong with Traddles is precisely that he is still wearing the same "old" watch; that is, Traddles, for the bulk of the novel, is very much stuck in time, a self-described "plodding kind of fellow" (383) for whom everything happens "after rather a long delay" (382), particularly his long-deferred marriage.

12. It is perhaps for this reason, this association with a grubbing middle class, that Steerforth, the one "Public School Man" in the novel, refuses to undergo the examination that will earn him a ranked degree. "'You'll take a high degree at college, Steerforth,'" David says to him, "'if you have not done so already; and they will have good reason to be proud of you!' '*I* take a degree!' cried Steerforth. 'Not I! my dear Daisy—will you mind my calling you Daisy? . . . 'I have not the least desire or intention to distinguish myself in

that way . . . why should I trouble myself, that a parcel of heavy-headed fellows may gape and hold up their hands?'" (276)

13. "'Procrastination is the thief of time'" (166), Mr. Micawber tells David. In always focusing on ends (money) and never on means (work), Mr. Micawber is as much a thief of time as the watch-stealing servant. More specifically, Mr. Micawber appropriates the time of his friend Traddles. Because he must make a certain amount of money in order to marry his sweetheart, Traddles thinks quite literally of his savings and investments in terms of buying time, bringing him closer in time to his future wife. When Mr. Micawber defaults on a loan he has asked Traddles to co-sign, forcing Traddles to forfeit his property, Micawber causes Traddles to lose the time he had "made" in his journey to marriage.

14. "Temporally," Patrick Brantlinger writes, "these new instruments of national debt and middle-class commerce were all future oriented" (22).

15. See Altick for a discussion of both the increasing public visibility of speculative pursuits in the mid-nineteenth century and Dickens's representations of these pursuits in his novels.

16. Joseph Payne is reported in the College of Preceptors minutes as saying, "he could not help thinking that many persons were going examination mad at the present moment" (qtd in Roach 268).

17. One sees the same collapse of time into mental property or capital in the following exchange between Francis Galton and his cousin Charles Darwin. After reading Galton's book *Hereditary Genius* (1872), Darwin wrote to him: "You have made a convert of an opponent in one sense, for I have always maintained that, excepting fools, men did not differ much in intellect, only in zeal and hard work." Galton replied: "Character, including the aptitude for hard work, is inheritable like every other faculty" (*Memories*).

18. In his essay "To Saunter, To Hurry: Dickens, Time, and Industrial Capitalism," N. N. Feltes also investigated the role of "factory time" in Dickens. He argued that Dickens attempted figuratively to resolve the conflict between laborers and the new time discipline by, among other things, representing Mr. Toodles in *Dombey and Son* as a man who "achieved equipoise" with mechanical labor. Feltes was not interested, however, in either the issue of intelligence or the problem of the professional.

19. "Novelists fighting for economic bargaining power in 1850," Lund wrote, "had given up a romantic notion of the writer as unconscious, effortless creator for the image of hard-working bourgeois businessman" (26). Lund provided a useful corrective to those critics quick to assume that the mid-nineteenth-century writer was as averse to the concept of waged or salaried labor as his earlier or later counterparts, but when he described the process as a straightforward substitution of one imaginary identity for another, he simplified what was in fact a complex, uneven, and contradictory process. Indeed, Lund simplified his own argument with its hints that the writer must identify as much as a "laborer" as he does as a "businessman." The Victorian writer did indeed reject the Romantic version of himself but in its place he substituted neither a laborer nor a businessman but an amalgam that rose above them both: the professional.

20. An author in the *National Magazine* wrote later in the decade, "Literary men . . . if we may judge by the sneers and innuendos of the press . . . have not a very high appreciation of total abstinence . . . [The literary men] will give to Bacchus the hours the mere man of business is devoting to his it may be ignoble yet useful calling" (19).

21. See Bruce Robbins's essay "Telescopic Philanthropy: Professionalism and Responsibility in *Bleak House*" for another perspective on the objectivity of professionals in Dickens.

22. See Anita Levy's essay "Gendered Labor, the Woman Writer and Dorothy Richardson" for what might be considered the evolution of this mid-nineteenth-century logic of professional domesticity. Levy argues that around the turn of the twentieth century both popular and modernist fiction depicted women who need to leave home and enter the professional world precisely so that they might qualify to *return* home.

23. My argument intersects with Nicholas Dames's on this point. Dames writes, "David's memory contains few seeds that fail to grow; very few events are without their companions and repetitions. The effect of all this chainlike concordance and integrity is, however, to reduce the capacity of experience to alter a life" (*Amnesiac Selves* 146).

Notes to Chapter Three

1. For discussions focused solely on the history of the examination, see Roach and Montgomery.

2: *The Times*'s interpretation exemplified this misunderstanding. On Feb. 9, 1854, it declared: "Nothing less is proposed than the creation of a new liberal profession, as freely open to all as the Church, the bar, of the hospital. From the time this measure receives the royal assent, it will be the fault of the people if the public service do not become their birthright, according to the talent, education, and industry of each, without any hindrance from those sinister influences which have hitherto, as a general rule, made access dependent on a powerful connexion or a seared conscience" (qtd. in Evans 113).

3. Nicholas Dames's "Trollope and the Career: Vocational Trajectories and the Management of Ambition" was published as I was revising this chapter. While not on *The Three Clerks*, in particular, Dames's argument about Trollope overlaps with mine on a number of points, though his tends to be framed in Foucauldian terms ("The figure of 'career,'" he writes, "managed to create linear, ordered sequences out of the disruptive energies unleashed by the spread of professionalism" (248)).

4. Charley's lack of grand ambition, his acceptance of himself as a mere hack, helps ensure his honesty. See Kucich for a discussion of the relationship between ambition and dishonesty in Trollope ("Transgression").

5. Since writing this, Lauren Goodlad's *Victorian Literature and the Victorian State* has appeared, which also offers an analysis of *The Three Clerks*, some of which overlaps with points I make here.

6. Recognizing this as central to Trollope's refusal of the logic of "unbought brains," Robert D. Aguirre writes in his excellent discussion of *An Autobiography*, "Trollope's accounting does not signal the failure of autobiography but the recognition of its inseparability from the material conditions of authorship itself" (569–70).

7. And Trollope has been called the "quintessential bourgeois" novelist (Praz 265).

Notes to Chapter Four

1. In 1997, Andrew Ross could yet write, "it is still a novelty to speak of academic labor" ("Labor behind the Cult of Work" 140), and, in 1998, Philip Altbach could still declare that although "there is a vague sense of unease," there is "little sense of crisis among

academics, and most are unaware of the magnitude of the problems facing American higher education" (113). In the last five years, however, an outpouring of books, articles, and even websites (see "workplace: a journal for academic labor" and "Invisible Adjunct") has polished our vague unease into hard concern.

2. "The literary and artistic world is so ordered that those who enter it have an interest in disinterestedness," he writes ("Field" 321).

3. I am indebted throughout my discussion of Woodmansee to Kaiser's excellent review.

4. George Levine makes a similar point when he comments at the beginning of *Dying to Know*, "I have found myself wanting to argue . . . that the hermeneutics of suspicion and the insistence on the primary values of localism and particularism have done what good work they can, and are now—often destructively—playing into the obsessive individualism of contemporary economic and social structures" (14).

5. In his introduction to *Day Late, Dollar Short; The Next Generation and the New Academy*, Peter C. Herman addresses both the new self-consciousness as well as its implicit voluntarism by observing, "there is the further irony in how the arguments for the importance (read continued funding) of the humanities often reiterate precisely the language that the new historicism and its allied approaches made so unstylish. Whereas the previous generation invented 'strategic essentialism,' the next generation might have to adopt 'strategic conservatism' simply in order to survive" (10). Unlike some other critics who have called for a reinvigorated formalism, Bell at least does admit that the solution is not to "resacraliz[e] the literary text" (488).

6. "Defensive interventions into the discourse of value, and . . . attempts to reclaim value by defining a new place for the aesthetic in contradistinction to the old conservative definitions of high culture," writes Isobel Armstrong, "would be regarded by Bourdieu as made possible by a number of related shifts in the field, opened up by, to hypothesize, mass education, global capital, post-modern repudiations of the grand narrative, and electronic media which have displaced the centrality of what we traditionally call the humanities" (*Radical Aesthetic* 155). See Harvey's *Condition of Postmodernity* for an account that explains the economic changes thoroughly and see Jameson's *Postmodernism* for one treating the cultural dynamic in more detail.

7. This move by which the politics of recent work is implicitly dismissed by linking it to the pressure of productivity is becoming common. Speaking of "the next generation" of literary critics, Jessie Swan claims that "for the sake of publishing . . . we are . . . pressured into the sexy over the arduous since we all can deconstruct, expose the dynamics of colonial power exploits, champion the subaltern, and reveal latent sexual desires in any text—from coupons to *Paradise Lost*—in far less time than it takes to understand the vicissitudes of the textual histories of authors and their work" (116). Geoffrey Galt Harpham, to take another example, follows a paragraph detailing recent criticism's domination "by sex, especially homosex; by race, especially minorities; by culture, especially material culture; by performance, especially the performance of identity" with one that makes the following statement: "literary scholars today don't feel the need to read anything else in literary studies—they just need to write" ("The End of Theory" 195).

8. Guillory's fatalism recalls Allen Dunn's argument about Bourdieu's sociology, the primary intellectual influence on Guillory. Dunn writes, "if there is a scandal to be found in Bourdieu's sociology of art, it is in the implication that we can attain freedom only by

assuming the position of spectators who witness the spectacle of human misery without being able to intervene, without being able to translate sociological knowledge into social practice" ("Who Needs a Sociology of the Aesthetic?" 90).

9. In yet another piece worrying about junior scholars who "reduce critical practice to exercises in political positioning," George Levine writes, "Literature remains a subject worth studying 'in its own right' (however complicated that idea has become)" ("Reclaiming the Aesthetic" 2,16). Levine distances himself from the very heart of his argument by placing "in its own right" in both scare quotes and giving it a self-conscious parenthetical. If, even as he argues for it, he is embarrassed by the idea that a critic could divorce a text from its material circumstances—studying it "in its own right"—then what chance do we as a profession have of recuperating this ideal in any sincere way?

10. Part of what I am trying to do is take seriously Kathleen McCormick's recent complaint that assessments of our "crisis" exhibit "a recurrent inability to engage dialectically with the past." She continues: "On the one hand there are those who seem to think that everything will be all right if we just go back. On the other, there are those, rather on the brink of despair, who seem quite sadly unable to find a way of redeeming the humanities. . . . Both of these perspectives are unable to find productive ways to understand the past in relation to the present" (137).

Works Cited

Ablow, Rachel. "Labors of Love: The Sympathetic Subjects of *David Copperfield*." *Dickens Studies Annual* 31 (2002): 23–46.

Ackroyd, Peter. *Dickens*. New York: HarperCollins, 1990.

Adams, James Eli. *Dandies and Desert Saints: Styles of Victorian Masculinity*. Ithaca, N.Y.: Cornell University Press, 1995.

———. "Recent Studies in the Nineteenth Century." *SEL: Studies in English Literature 1500–1900*. 41.4 (2001): 827–79.

Adorno, Theodor. *Aesthetic Theory*. Trans. C. Lenhardt. Ed. Gretel Adorno and Rolf Tiedeman. London: Routledge, 1970.

Aguirre, Robert D. "Cold Print: Professing Authorship in Anthony Trollope's *An Autobiography*." *Biography* 25.4 (2002): 569–92.

Altbach, Philip. "An International Academic Crisis? The American Professoriate in Comparative Perspective." *Forum Futures 1998*. Ed. Maureen E. Devlin and Joel W. Meyerson. Forum for the Future of Higher Education. Forum Strategy Series. 100–120.

Altick, Richard. "Education, Print, and Paper in *Our Mutual Friend*." In *Nineteenth Century Literary Perspectives; Essays in Honor of Lionel Stevenson*. Durham. N.C.: Duke University Press, 1974. 237–54.

———. "Speculation and Bankruptcy." In *The Presence of the Past*. Columbus: The Ohio State University Press, 1991. 638–67.

American Association of University Professors (AAUP). "Contingent Faculty Appointments." http://www.aaup.org/ISSUES/part-time/index/htm.

Anderson, Amanda. *The Powers of Distance: Cosmopolitanism and the Cultivation of Detachment*. Princeton, N.J.: Princeton University Press, 2001.

Annan, Noel. "The Intellectual Aristocracy." *Studies in Social History: A Tribute to G. M. Trevelyan*. Ed. J. H. Plumb. London: Longmans, Green and Co., 1955. 243–87.

Anonymous. "Competitive Examinations." *Cornhill Magazine* 4 (1861): 692–712.

Armstrong, Isobel. *The Radical Aesthetic*. Oxford: Blackwell Press, 2000.

Armstrong, Nancy. *Desire and Domestic Fiction*. Oxford: Oxford University Press, 1987.

Armstrong, Nancy and Leonard Tennenhouse. "The Vanishing Intellectual." In *The Imaginary Puritan: Literature, Intellectual Labor, and the Origins of Personal Life*. Berkeley: University of California Press, 1992. 114–39.

Arnold, Matthew. "The Function of Criticism at the Present Time." *Poetry and Criticism of Matthew Arnold*. Ed. A. Dwight Culler. Boston: Houghton Mifflin, 1961. 237–58.

Aronowitz, Stanley. *The Knowledge Factory: Dismantling the Corporate University and Creating True Higher Learning*. Boston: Beacon Press, 2001.

———. "On Intellectuals." *Intellectuals: Aesthetics, Politics, Academics*. Ed. Bruce Robbins. Minneapolis: University of Minnesota Press, 1990.

Barrett, Dorothea. *Vocation and Desire: George Eliot's Heroines*. London: Routledge, 1989.

Baumgarten, Murray. "Railway/Reading/Time." *Dickens Studies Annual* 19 (1990): 65–89.

Bell, David. "A Moratorium on Suspicion?" *PMLA* 117.3 (2002): 487–89.

Benson, Arthur Christopher, and Viscount Esther. *The Letters of Queen Victoria*. London: John Murray, 1908.

Bérubé, Michael. "Days of Future Past." *ADE Bulletin* 131 (Spring): 20–26.

———. *The Employment of English: Theory, Jobs, and the Future of Literary Studies*. New York: NYU Press, 1998.

Bourdieu, Pierre. *Distinction: A Social Critique of the Judgment of Taste*. Trans. Richard Nice. Cambridge, Mass.: Harvard University Press, 1984.

———. "The Field of Cultural Production, or: The Economic World Reversed." *Poetics* 12 (1983): 241–58.

———. "The Forms of Capital." In *Handbook of Theory and Research for the Sociology of Education*. Ed. John G. Richardson. New York: Greenwood, 1986. 241–59.

———. *The Field of Cultural Production*. New York: Columbia University Press, 1993.

———. *Pascalian Meditations*. Trans. Richard Nice. Stanford, Calif.: Stanford University Press, 2000.

———. *Practical Reason: On the Theory of Action*. Stanford, Calif.: Stanford University Press, 1998.

———. "The Production of Belief: Contribution to an Economy of Symbolic Goods." *Media, Culture, and Society* 2.3 (1980): 261–93.

——— and Jean-Claude Passeron. *Reproduction in Education, Society, and Culture*. Trans. Richard Nice. London: SAGE Publications, 1977.

———. *The Rules of Art: Genesis and Structure of the Literary Field*. Trans. Susan Emanuel. Stanford, Calif.: Stanford University Press, 1996.

———. "Social Space and Symbolic Power." *In Other Words*. Trans. Matthew Adamson. Stanford, Calif.: Stanford University Press, 1990. 123–39.

———. *The State Nobility*. Trans. Lauretta C. Clough. Stanford, Calif.: Stanford University Press, 1996.

———. "Structures, Habitus, Power: Basis for a Theory of Symbolic Power." In *Culture/Power/History*. Ed. Nicholas B. Dirk et al. Princeton, N.J.: Princeton University Press, 1994. 155–99.

Bousquet, Marc. "The Rhetoric of 'Job Market' and the Reality of the Academic Labor System." *College English* 66.2 (November 2003): 207–28.

———. "The Waste Product of Graduate Education: Toward a Dictatorship of the Flexible." *Social Text* 20.1 (2002): 81–104.

Brantlinger, Patrick. *Fictions of State: Culture and Credit in Britain, 1694–1994*. Ithaca, N.Y.: Cornell University Press, 1996.

Braverman, Harry. *Labor and Monopoly Capital: The Degradation of Work in the Twentieth Century*. New York: Monthly Review Press, 1974.

Breneman, David W. "Alternatives to Tenure for the Next Generation of Academics." *Working Paper 8*. American Association for Higher Education. Washington, D.C., April 1, 1997.

Brontë, Charlotte. *The Professor.* 1847; reprint, London: Penguin Books, 1989.

Brown, Nicholas and Imre Szeman, eds. *Pierre Bourdieu: Fieldwork in Culture.* New York: Rowman and Littlefield, 2000.

Bürger, Peter. *The Theory of the Avante-Garde.* Trans. Michael Shaw. Minneapolis: University of Minnesota Press, 1984.

Chandler, James. "Critical Disciplinarity." *Critical Inquiry* 30.2 (Winter 2004): 355–60.

Christopher, Renny. "What about the Dumb Kids?" *the minnesota review* 61–62 (2004): 111–14.

Clarke, Edwin and L. S. Jacyna. *Nineteenth-Century Origins of Neuroscientific Concepts.* Berkeley: University of California Press, 1987.

Clarke, John. *New Times and Old Enemies: Essays on Cultural Studies and America.* London: HarperCollins Academic, 1991.

Cohen, Emmeline W. *The Growth of the British Civil Service, 1780–1939.* London: Frank Cass & Co. Ltd., 1965.

Cohen, Monica Feinberg. *Professional Domesticity in the Victorian Novel.* Cambridge: Cambridge University Press, 1998.

Coleman, Jon T. "Just Deserts s." *Chronicle of Higher Education* Sept. 17, 2004, C3.

"Competitive Examinations." *Nature* 10 (Sept. 1874): 416–18.

Cooter, Roger. *The Cultural Meaning of Popular Science; Phrenology and the Organization of Consent in Nineteenth-Century Britain.* Cambridge: Cambridge University Press, 1984.

Cordery, Gareth. "Foucault, Dickens, and David Copperfield." *Victorian Literature and Culture* 26.1 (1998): 71–85.

Cottom, Daniel. *Social Figures; George Eliot, Social History, and Literary Representation.* Minneapolis: University of Minnesota Press, 1987.

Crosby, Christina. "Trollope's Addictive Realism." In *The New Economic Criticism: Studies at the Intersection of Literature and Economics.* Ed. Martha Woodmansee and Mark Osteen. New York: Routledge, 1999. 293–305.

D'Albertis, Deidre. "'Bookmaking Out of the Remains of the Dead': Elizabeth Gaskell's *The Life of Charlotte Brontë.*" *Victorian Studies* 39.1 (Autumn 1995): 1–31.

Dallas, E. S. Review 1859. In *Trollope: The Critical Heritage.* Ed. Donald Smalley. London: Routledge, 1969. 103–9.

Dames, Nicholas. *Amnesiac Selves: Nostalgia, Forgetting, and British Fiction, 1810–1870.* Oxford: Oxford University Press, 2001.

———. "The Clinical Novel: Phrenology and *Villette.*" *Novel* 29.3 (1996): 367–90.

———. "Trollope and the Career: Vocational Trajectories and the Management of Ambition." *Victorian Studies* 45.2 (Winter 2003): 247–78.

Danahy, Paul. *A Community of One: Masculine Autobiography and Autonomy in Nineteenth-Century Britain.* Binghamton: SUNY Press, 1993.

Darwin, Bernard. *The Dickens Advertiser.* New York: Haskell House, 1930.

Daston, Lorraine and Peter Galison. "The Image of Objectivity." *Representations* 40 (1992): 80–128.

"A Daughter of the Camp." *Punch.* V.25 (July to Dec. 1853).

Davidoff, Leonore and Catherine Hall. *Family Fortunes.* Chicago: University of Chicago Press, 1991.

Delany, Paul. *Literature, Money, and the Market: From Trollope to Amis.* New York: Palgrave, 2002.

Dickens, Charles. *David Copperfield.* 1847–50; reprint, Hertfordshire: Wordsworth Classics, 1992.

———. *Great Expectations.* 1861; reprint, Boston: Bedford Books, 1996.

Dillon, Steven. "Illustrations of Time: Watches, Dials, and Clocks in Victorian Pictures." In *The Victorian Illustrated Book.* Ed. Richard Maxwell. Charlottesville: University of Virginia Press, 2002. 52–90.

DiMaggio, Paul. "Social Structure, Institutions, and Cultural Goods: The Case of the U.S." In *The Politics of Culture: Policy Perspectives for Individuals, Institutions, and Communities.* Ed. Gigi Bradford et al. New York: The New Press, 2000.

Dunn, Allen. "Who Needs a Sociology of the Aesthetic? Freedom and Value in Bourdieu's *Rules of Art.*" *boundary 2* 25.1 (Spring 1998): 87–110.

———. "Review of *Pierre Bourdieu: Fieldwork in Culture.*" *symploke* 9.1–2 (2001): 202–4.

Durkheim, Emile. *The Division of Labor in Society.* New York: Free Press: 1997.

Dweck, Carol S. *Self-Theories: Their Role in Motivation, Personality, and Development.* Philadelphia: Taylor and Francis, 2000.

Dyson, A. E., and Julian Lovelock. *Education and Democracy.* London: Routledge, 1975.

Eagleton, Terry. "Class, Power, and Charlotte Brontë." Rpt. in *Critical Essays on Charlotte Brontë.* Ed. Barbara Timm Gates. Boston: G.K. Hall & Co., 1990. 50–59.

Ehrenreich, Barbara and John Ehrenreich. "The Professional-Managerial Class." In *Between Labor and Capital.* Ed. Pat Walker. Boston: South End Press, 1979. 5–45.

Eliot, George. *Middlemarch: A Study of Provincial Life.* 1872; reprint, New York: Penguin, 1981.

English, James. "Winning the Culture Game: Prizes, Awards, and the Rules of Art." *New Literary History* 33.1 (2002): 109–35.

Evans, Eric J. *Social Policy 1830–1914: Individualism, Collectivism, and the Origins of the Welfare State.* London: Routledge, 1978.

"Faculty Openings in English, Foreign Languages Drop Sharply." *Chronicle of Higher Education,* December 16, 2002.

Feltes, N. N. "To Saunter, To Hurry: Dickens, Time, and Industrial Capitalism." *Victorian Studies* 20 (1977): 245–67.

Fish, Stanley. "Authors-Readers: Jonson's Community of the Same." *Representations* 7 (Summer 1984): 26–58.

———. "The Unbearable Ugliness of Volvos." In *There is No Such Thing as Free Speech; and It's a Good Thing, Too.* New York: Oxford University Press, 1994. 273–79.

Florida, Richard. *The Rise of the Creative Class.* New York: Basic Books, 2002.

Freedman, Jonathan. *Professions of Taste: Henry James, British Aestheticism, and Commodity Culture.* Stanford, Calif.: Stanford University Press, 1990.

Foucault, Michel. *Discipline and Punish.* New York: Vintage, 1979.

———. *The History of Sexuality,* Vol. 1. Trans. Robert Hurley. New York: Vintage, 1990.

Friedson, Eliot. "The Futures of Professionalization." In *Health and the Division of Labour.* Ed. Margaret Stacey et al. London: Croom, 1977. 14–40.

Froude, J. A. *The Nemesis of Faith.* 2nd ed. London: John Chapman, 1849.

Frow, John. *Cultural Studies and Cultural Value.* Oxford: Oxford University Press, 1995.

Galton, Sir Francis. *Hereditary Genius; An Inquiry into Its Laws and Consequences.* 1869; reprint, New York: Horizon Press, 1952.

———. *Memories of My Life.* 2nd ed. London: Methuen, 1908.

Gappa, Judith M. and Shelly M. MacDermid. "Work, Family, and the Faculty Career." AAHE Working Paper Series, Inquiry #8, 1997.

Gérin, Winifred. *Charlotte Brontë: The Evolution of Genius.* Oxford: Oxford University Press, 1966.

Gladwell, Malcolm. "The Talent Myth." *New Yorker*, July 22, 2002. 28–33.

Glen, Heather. "Introduction." Charlotte Brontë, *The Professor.* London: Penguin Books, 1989.

Goodlad, Lauren. "'A Middle Class Cut into Two': Historiography and Victorian National Character." *ELH* 67.1 (2000): 143–78.

———. *Victorian Culture and the Victorian State.* Baltimore, Md.: Johns Hopkins University Press, 2003.

Gould, Stephen Jay. *The Mismeasure of Man.* New York: Norton, 1981.

Greenstein, Michael. "Measuring Time in *Dombey and Son.*" *Dickens Quarterly* 9 (1992): 151–57.

Gregory, Christian. "The Future of an Illusion." *Workplace.* www.workplace gsc.com/features1/gregory.html

Griffin, Lepel. "Indian Civil Service Examinations." *Fortnightly Review* XXIII (1875): 522–36.

Guillory, John. "Bourdieu's Refusal." *MLQ* 58:4 (1997): 367–98

———. "Critical Response: The Name of Science, the Name of Politics." *Critical Inquiry* 29 (Spring 2003): 526–41.

———. *Cultural Capital: The Problem of Literary Canon Formation.* Chicago: University of Chicago Press, 1993.

———. "From High Theory to Low Theory: The Succession of Cultural Studies." Talk given at Portland State University, April 24, 2000.

———. "Literary Critics as Intellectuals: Class Analysis and the Crisis of the Humanities." In *Rethinking Class: Literary Studies and Social Formations.* Ed. Wai Chee Dimock and Michael T. Gilmore. New York: Columbia University Press, 1994. 107–48.

———. "Preprofessionalism: What Graduate Students Want." *ADE Bulletin* 113 (Spring 1996): 4–8.

Habermas, Jürgen. *The Philosophical Discourse of Modernity: Twelve Lectures.* Boston: MIT Press, 1990.

Hack, Daniel. "Literary Paupers and Professional Authors: The Guild of Literature and Art." *SEL: Studies in English Literature 1500–1900* 39.4 (1999): 691–713.

———. *The Material Interests of the Victorian Novel.* Forthcoming (Charlotte: University of Virginia Press).

Hall, Oswald. "The Informal Organization of Medical Practice in an American City." Excerpted in *Professionalization.* Ed. Howard M. Vollmer and Donald L. Mills. Englewood Cliffs, N.J.: Prentice-Hall, 1966. 88–97.

Hamer, Mary. Writing By Numbers: Trollope's Serial Fiction. Cambridge: Cambridge University Press, 1987.

Hardt, Michael. "Affective Immaterial Labor." *boundary 2* 26.2 (Summer 1999): 89–100.

Harpham, Geoffrey Galt. "The End of Theory, The Rise of Professionalism." In *Professions: Conversations on the Future of Literary and Cultural Studies.* Ed. Donald E. Hall. Chicago: University of Illinois Press, 2001. 186–201.

———. "Aesthetics and the Fundamentals of Modernity." *Aesthetics and Ideology.* New Brunswick, N.J.: Rutgers University Press, 1994. 124–49.

Harrington, Anne. *Medicine, Mind, and the Double Brain.* Princeton, N.J.: Princeton University Press, 1987.

Harris, Charles B. "The Downsizing of the American Mind." *ADE Bulletin* 121 (Winter 1998): 25–28.

Harvey, David. *The Condition of Postmodernity.* Cambridge: Blackwell, 1989.

———. *The Limits to Capital.* Chicago: University of Chicago Press, 1982.

Herman, Deborah M. and Julie Schmid, eds. *Cogs in the Classroom Factory: The Changing Identity of Academic Labor.* London: Praeger, 2003.

Herman, Peter C. "60s Theory/90s Practice." In *Day Late, Dollar Short: The Next Generation and the New Academy.* Albany: SUNY Press, 2000. 1–24.

Heyck, T. W. *The Transformation of Intellectual Life in Victorian England.* New York: St. Martin's, 1982.

Hoberek, Andrew. "Professionalism: What Graduate Students Need." *symploke* 10.1 (2002): 52–70.

Hodges, Donald Clark. *Class Politics in the Information Age.* Chicago: University of Illinois Press, 2000.

Hope, Keith. *The Political Conception of Merit.* Forthcoming from Russell Sage.

House, Humphry. *The Dickens World.* London: Oxford University Press, 1960.

House, Madeline, Graham Storey, and Kathleen Tillotson, eds. *The Letters of Charles Dickens.* Oxford: Clarendon Press, 1988. 10 vols.

Hughes, Edward. "Sir Charles Trevelyan and Civil Service Reform, 1853–5." *English Historical Review* 64 (1949): 3–88; 206–34.

Hughes, Linda and Michael Lund. *The Victorian Serial.* Charlottesville: University of Virginia Press, 1991.

Jameson, Fredric. *The Cultural Turn.* London: Verso, 1998.

———. *The Political Unconscious: Narrative as a Socially Symbolic Act.* Ithaca, N.Y.: Cornell University Press, 1981.

———. *Postmodernism: Or, The Cultural Logic of Late Capitalism.* Durham, N.C.: Duke University Press, 1991.

———. "Reification and Utopia in Mass Culture." *Social Text* 1 (1979): 130–48.

———. "The Theoretical Hesitation: Benjamin's Sociological Predecessor." *Critical Inquiry* 25 (Winter 1999): 267–86.

———. "The Vanishing Mediator; or, Max Weber as Storyteller." In *The Ideologies of Theory,* Vol. 2. Minneapolis: University of Minnesota Press, 1988. 3–34.

Johnson, Benjamin, Patrick Kavanagh, and Kevin Mattson. *Steal This University: The Rise of the Corporate University and the Academic Labor Movement.* New York: Routledge, 2003.

Kaiser, David Aram. "Whither Kantian Aesthetics?" *Eighteenth-Century Life* 20.1 (1996): 101–8.

Kamin, Leon J. *The Science and Politics of IQ.* Harmondsworth: Penguin, 1977.

Kincaid, James. "Anthony Trollope and the Unmannerly Novel." In *Reading and Writing Women's Lives: A Study of the Novel of Manners.* Ed. Bege Bowers and Barbara Brothers. Ann Arbor, Mich.: UMI Research Project, 1990. 87–104.

Kirkpatrick, David D. "'Oprah' Gaffe by Franzen Draws Ire and Sales." *New York Times* 21 Oct. 2001.

Kreilkamp, Ivan. "Victorian Poetry's Modernity." *Victorian Poetry* 41.4 (2003): 603–11.

Kucich, John. *Cambridge Companion to the Victorian Novel.* Cambridge: Cambridge University Press, 2003.

———. "Transgression in Trollope: Dishonesty and the Antibourgeois Elite." *ELH* 56 (1989): 593–616.

Lambert, Gregg. "'What does ~~woman~~ graduate students want?' John Guillory and the Obscure Object of Desire." *the minnesota review* n.s. 52–54 (2001). 249–62.

Lane, Christopher. *The Burdens of Intimacy: Psychoanalysis and Victorian Masculinity.* Chicago: University of Chicago Press, 1999.

Larson, Magali Sarfatti. *The Rise of Professionalism: A Sociological Analysis.* Berkeley: University of California Press, 1977.

Laurence, David. "The Latest Forecast." *ADE Bulletin* 131 (Spring 2002): 15–19.

Lemann, Nicholas. *The Big Test: The Secret History of the American Meritocracy.* New York: Farrar, Straus, and Giroux, 1999.

Levine, George. "Aesthetics and Ideology Revisited." *Contemporary Literature* 41.4 (Winter 2000): 748–70.

———. *Dying to Know.* Chicago: University of Chicago Press, 2002.

———. "Reclaiming the Aesthetic." *Aesthetics and Ideology.* New Brunswick, N.J.: Rutgers University Press, 1994. 1–28.

———. "The Two Nations." *Pedagogy* 1.1 (2001): 7–19.

Levy, Anita. "Gendered Labor, the Woman Writer, and Dorothy Richardson." *Novel* 24 (1991): 50–70.

———. *Reproductive Urges: Popular Novel Reading, Sexuality, and the English Nation.* Princeton, N.J.: Princeton University Press, 1999.

Lloyd, David. "Analogies of the Aesthetic: The Politics of Culture and the Limits of Materialist Aesthetics." In *New Formations.* London: Methuen, 1987.

——— and Paul Thomas. *Culture and the State.* New York: Routledge, 1998.

Lubenow, W. C. *The Cambridge Apostles, 1820–1914: Liberalism, Imagination, and Friendship in British Intellectual and Professional Life.* Cambridge: Cambridge University Press, 1998.

Lukács, Georg. "Reification and the Consciousness of the Proletariat." In *History and Class Consciousness: Studies in Marxist Dialectics.* Trans. Rodney Livingstone. Cambridge, Mass.: MIT Press, 1971. 83–221.

Lund, Michael. "Novels, Writers, and Readers in 1850." *Victorian Periodicals Review* 17 (1984): 15–28.

Macdonald, Keith. *Sociological Analysis of the Novel Professions.* London: Sage, 1995.

Marcuse, Herbert. "The Affirmative Character of Culture." In *Negations.* Trans. Jeremy Shapiro. Boston: Beacon Press, 1968. 88–133.

Martin, Bill, and Ivan Szelényi. "Beyond Cultural Capital: Toward a Theory of Symbolic Domination." In *Intellectuals, Universities, and the State in Western Modern Societies.* Berkeley: University of California Press. 16–49.

Marx, Karl. *Capital; A Critique of Political Economy.* Ed. Frederick Engels. New York: International, 1967. 3 vols.

———. "Estranged Labor." In *Economic and Philosophic Manuscripts of 1844.* Ed. Dirk J. Struik. New York: International, 1964.

McCormick, Kathleen. "Finding Hope in the Humanities." *College Literature* 28.3 (Fall 2001): 129–40.

McGee, Micki. "Hooked on Higher Education and Other Tales from Adjunct Faculty Organizing." *Social Text* 20.1 (2002): 61–80.

McGowan, John (with Regenia Gagnier). "Intellectual Work Today: Some Trans-Atlantic Musings." In *Novel Professions: Conversations on the Future of Literary and Cultural Studies.* Ed. Donald E. Hall. Chicago: University of Illinois Press, 2001. 37–59.

McLaughlin, Kevin. *Writing in Parts: Imitation and Exchange in Nineteenth-Century Literature.* Stanford, Calif.: Stanford University Press, 1995.

Mill, John Stuart. "Thoughts on Parliamentary Reform." 1859. In *Collected Works of John Stuart Mill.* Vol. 19. Toronto: University of Toronto Press, 1977. 313–39.

Miller, Andrew. "Owning Up; Possessive Individualism in Trollope's *Autobiography* and *The Eustace Diamonds.*" In *Novels behind Glass.* Cambridge: Cambridge University Press, 159–88.

———. "Recent Studies in the Nineteenth Century." *SEL* 43.4 (Autumn 2003): 959–1017.

Miller, D. A. "Secret Subjects, Open Secrets." In *The Novel and the Police.* Berkeley: University of California Press, 1988.

Mintz, Alan L. *George Eliot and the Novel of Vocation.* Cambridge, Mass.: Harvard University Press, 1978.

Moi, Toril. "The Challenge of the Particular Case: Bourdieu's Sociology of Culture and Literary Criticism." *MLQ* 58.4 (Dec. 1997): 497–508.

Montgomery, R. J. *Examinations: An Account of Their Evolution as Administrative Devices in England.* Pittsburgh, Penn.: University of Pittsburgh Press, 1965.

Moretti, Franco. "The Comfort of Civilization." *Representations* 12 (Fall 1985): 115–39.

Morison, James Cotter. "Isaac Casaubon." *Fortnightly Review* XXIII (1875): 537–51.

Morris, Pam. "*Bleak House* and the Struggle for the State Domain." *ELH* 68.3 (2001): 679–98.

Moses, Robert. *The Civil Service of Great Britain.* New York: AMS Press, 1966.

Mueller, Hans-Eberhard. *Bureaucracy, Education, and Monopoly: Civil Service Reforms in Prussia and England.* Berkeley: University of California Press, 1984.

Negri, Antonio. "Value and Affect." *boundary 2* 26.2 (Summer 1999): 77–89.

Newman, Karen. "Nice Work If We Can Keep It." *Academe* (May–June 1999): 29–33.

Newman, Neville. "Workers, Gentleman, and Landowners: Identifying Social Class in *The Professor* and *Wuthering Heights.*" *Brontë Society Transactions* 26.1 (April 2001): 10–18.

Nicholls, John G. "Effort Is Virtuous, But It's Better to Have Ability: Evaluative Responses to Perceptions of Effort and Ability." *Journal of Research in Personality* 10 (1976): 306–15.

Noble, David F. "Digital Diploma Mills." In *Steal This University.* Ed. Benjamin Johnson et al., N.Y.: Routledge, 2003. 33–48.

———. *Digital Diploma Mills: The Automation of Higher Education.* New York: Monthly Review Press, 2002.

Nunokawa, Jeff. "Eros and Isolation: The Antisocial George Eliot." *ELH* 69.4 (2002): 835–60.

O'Connor, Erin. "Introduction." *On Scholarly Love.* Dec. 27, 2003. www.erinoconnor.org/writing/scholarlylove.shtml

Parliamentary Papers. Government; Civil Service 2. Shannon: Irish University Press Series, 1969.

Parsons, Talcott. "The Professions and Social Structure." 1939. Reprinted in *Professionalization.* Ed. Howard M. Vollmer and Donald L. Mills. Englewood Cliffs, N.J.: Prentice-Hall, 1966. 56–58

Patten, Robert L. *Charles Dickens and His Publishers.* Oxford: Clarendon, 1978.

Paulson, William. *Literary Culture in a World Transformed: A Future for the Humanities.* Ithaca, N.Y.: Cornell University Press, 2001.

———. "The Market of Printed Goods: On Bourdieu's Rules." *MLQ* 58:4 (1997). 399–415.

Peacock, Thomas Love. *Headlong Hall and Gryll Grange.* Oxford: Oxford University Press, 1987. 89–322.

Perkin, Harold. *Origins of Modern English Society.* London: Routledge, 1969.

———. *The Rise of Professional Society.* London: Routledge, 1989.

Peterson, M. Jeanne. *The Medical Profession in Mid-Victorian England.* Berkeley: University of California Press, 1978.

"A Phrenological Puzzle" *Punch* V.25 (July to Dec. 1853).

Pettitt, Clare. *Patent Inventions: Intellectual Property and the Victorian Novel.* Oxford: Oxford University Press, 2004.

Pfau, Thomas. *Wordsworth's Profession: Form, Class, and the Logic of Early Romantic Cultural Production.* Stanford, Calif.: Stanford University Press, 1997.

Poovey, Mary. "Aesthetics and Political Economy in the Eighteenth Century: The Place of Gender in the Social Constitution of Knowledge." In *Aesthetics and Ideology.* Ed. George Levine. New Brunswick, N.J.: Rutgers University Press, 1994. 79–105.

———. "Beyond the Literary-Critical Impasse." *American Literary Quarterly* 11.2 (Summer 1999): 354–77.

———. *A History of the Modern Fact.* Chicago: University of Chicago Press, 1998.

———. "The Man-of-Letters Hero: *David Copperfield* and the Professional Writer." In *Uneven Developments.* Chicago: University of Chicago Press, 1988. 89–125.

———. "The Twenty-First Century University and the Market: What Price Economic Viability?" *differences* 12.1 (2001): 1–16.

"The Position of Men in Letters." *The National Magazine* (1858–1860).

Poulantzas, Nicos. *Classes in Contemporary Capitalism.* Trans. David Fernbach. London: Verso, 1975.

Pratt, Linda Ray. "Going Public: Political Discourse and the Faculty Voice." In *Higher Education under Fire.* Ed. Cary Nelson and Michael Bérubé. London: Routledge, 1995. 35–51.

Praz, Mario. *The Hero in Eclipse in Victorian Fiction.* Trans. Angus Davidson. Oxford: Oxford University Press, 1956.

Psomiades, Kathy. *Beauty's Body: Femininity and Representation in British Aestheticism.* Stanford, Calif.: Stanford University Press, 1997.

Rabinbach, Anson. *The Human Motor.* Berkeley: University of California Press, 1990.

Rancière, Jacques. "The Aesthetic Revolution and Its Outcomes." *New Left Review* (March/April 2002): 133–51.

Rauch, Alan. "Lessons Learned in Class: Charlotte Brontë's *The Professor.*" In *Useful Knowledge: The Victorians, Morality, and the March of Intellect.* Durham, N.C.: Duke University, Press, 2001. 129–63.

Readings, Bill. *The University in Ruins.* Cambridge, Mass.: Harvard University Press, 1996.

Reader, W. J. *Professional Men: The Rise of the Professional Classes in Nineteenth-Century England.* New York: Basic Books, 1966.

Reich, Robert B. *The Next American Frontier.* New York: Times Books, 1983.

———. *The Future of Success: Working and Living in the New Economy.* New York: Vintage, 2002.

Review of *The Three Clerks. Spectator* (1875). In *Trollope: The Critical Heritage.* Ed. Donald Smalley. London: Routledge, 1969. 59–60.

Rhoades, Gary. *Managed Professionals: Unionized Faculty and Restructuring Academic Labor.* Albany: SUNY Press, 1998.

Richards, Graham. *Mental Machinery: The Origins and Consequences of Psychological Ideas.* Part 1. *1600–1850.* London: The Athlone Press, 1992.

Roach, John. *Public Examinations in England, 1850–1900.* Cambridge: Cambridge University Press, 1971.

Robbins, Bruce, ed. *Intellectuals: Aesthetics, Politics, Academics.* Minneapolis: University of Minnesota Press, 1990.

———. "Less Disciplinary Than Thou: Criticism and the Conflict of the Faculties." *the minnesota review* 45–46 (1995–96).

———. *Secular Vocations: Intellectuals, Professionalism, Culture.* London: Verso, 1993.

———. "Telescopic Philanthropy: Professionalism and Responsibility in *Bleak House.*" In *Nation and Narration.* Ed. Homi K. Bhabha. New York: Routledge, 1990. 213–30.

———. "The Village of the Liberal-Managerial Class." In *Cosmopolitan Geographies.* Ed. Vinay Dharwadker. New York: Routledge, 2001. 15–32.

Ross, Andrew. "The Mental Labor Problem." *Social Text* 18.2 (2000): 1–31.

———. "The Labor behind the Cult of Work." In *Will Teach for Food: Academic Labor in Crisis.* Ed. Cary Nelson. Minneapolis: University of Minnesota Press, 1997. 137–43.

Rothfield, Lawrence. *Vital Signs: Medical Realism in Nineteenth-Century Fiction.* Princeton, N.J.: Princeton University Press, 1992.

Ruth, Jennifer. "The Case of *The Zooist.*" *Victorian Periodicals Review* 32.4 (1998): 299–323.

———. "The Self-Sacrificing Professional: Dickens's 'Hunted Down' and *A Tale of Two Cities.*" *Dickens Studies Annual* 34 (2004): 283–99.

Sayce, A. H. "The Results of the Examination-System at the Universities." *Fortnightly Review* XXIII (1875): 835–46.

Schaffer, Simon. "Babbage's Intelligence: Calculating Engines and the Factory System." *Critical Inquiry* (Autumn 1994): 203–27.

Searle, G. R. *Entrepreneurial Politics in Mid-Victorian Britain.* Oxford: Oxford University Press, 1993.

Sedgwick, Eve. *Epistemology of the Closet.* Berkeley: University of California Press, 1990.

Seltzer, Mark. *Henry James and the Art of Power.* Ithaca, N.Y.: Cornell University Press, 1984.

Shapin, Steven. "Phrenological Knowledge and the Social Structure in Early Nineteenth Century Edinburgh." *Annals of Science* 32.3 (1975): 219–43.

Sherman, Stuart. *Telling Time: Clocks, Diaries, and Diurnal Forms.* Chicago: University of Chicago Press, 1996.

Sherry, Norman. *Charlotte and Emily Brontë.* New York: Arco, 1970.

Shuman, Cathy. "Invigilating *Our Mutual Friend:* Gender and the Professional Legitimation of Authority." *Novel* 28 (1995): 154–72.

———. "Laborer and Hire: Trollope, Northcote-Trevelyan, and *The Three Clerks.*" In *Pedagogical Economies: The Examination and the Victorian Literary Man.* Stanford, Calif.: Stanford University Press, 2000. 76–122.

Shuttleworth, Sally. *Charlotte Brontë and Victorian Psychology.* Cambridge: Cambridge University Press, 1996.

Siskin, Clifford. *The Work of Writing: Literature and Social Change in Britain, 1700–1830.* New York: Oxford University Press, 1998.

Slaughter, Sheila. *Academic Capitalism: Politics, Policies, and the Entrepreneurial University.* Baltimore, Md.: Johns Hopkins University Press, 1999.

Smith, Barbara Herrnstein. *Contingencies of Value.* Cambridge, Mass.: Harvard University Press, 1988.

Stafford, Margot. "Keeping One's Own Counsel: Authorship, Literary Advice, and *New Gen Street. Gissing Journal* 37 (April 2001): 1–18.

Stolnitz, Jerome. "On the Origins of 'Aesthetic Disinterestedness.'" *The Journal of Aesthetics and Art Criticism* 20 (Winter 1961): 131–43.

Sturt, Mary. *Education of the People; A History of Primary Education in England and Wales in the Nineteenth Century.* London: Routledge, 1967.

Super, R. H. "Trollope at the Royal Literary Fund." *Nineteenth-Century Fiction* 37.3 (Dec. 1982): 316–28.

Sutherland, Gillian. *Ability, Merit, and Measurement.* Oxford: Oxford University Press, 1984.

Sutherland, J. A. *Victorian Novelists and Publishers.* Chicago: University of Chicago Press, 1976.

Swan, Jessie G. "Breaking the Monopoly: The Next Generation and the Corporate Academy." *Day Late, Dollar Short; The Next Generation and the New Academy.* Ed. Peter C. Herman. New York: SUNY Press, 2000. 113–27.

Thackeray, William Makepeace. 1850; reprint, *The History of Pendennis.* Harmondsworth: Penguin, 1972.

Thomas, David Wayne. *Cultivating Victorians: Liberal Culture and the Aesthetic.* Philadelphia: University of Pennsylvania Press, 2004.

Thompson, E. P. "Time, Work-Discipline, and Industrial Capitalism." In *Customs in Common.* New York: New Press, 1990. 352–403.

Thomson, H. Byerley. *The Choice of a Profession.* London, 1857.

Titolo, Matthew. "The Clerk's Tale: Liberalism, Accountability, and Mimesis in *David Copperfield.*" *ELH* 70 (Spring 2003): 171–95.

Tirelli, Vincent. "Adjuncts and More Adjuncts: Labor Segmentation and the Transformation of Higher Education." In *Chalk Lines: The Politics of Work in the Managed University.* Ed. Randy Martin. Durham, N.C.: Duke University Press, 1998. 181–201.

Trollope, Anthony. *Barchester Towers.* 1857; reprint, Oxford: Oxford University Press, 1998.

———. *The Three Clerks.* Ed. Graham Handley. 1857; reprint, Oxford: Oxford University Press, 1989.

———. "The Civil Service as Profession." *Cornhill Magazine* 3 (1861): 214–28.

———. *Autobiography.* London: Williams & Norgate, 1946.

Veblen, Thorstein. "The Place of Science in Modern Civilization." 1980; reprinted in T. Veblen, *The Place of Science in Modern Civilization and Other Esssays.* London: Transactional Publishers, 1990.

Vrettos, Athena. "Defining Habits: Dickens and the Psychology of Repetition." *Victorian Studies* 42.3 (Spring 2000): 399–426.

Walker, Pat, ed. *Between Labor and Capital.* Boston: South End Press, 1979.

Wallerstein, Immanuel. "The Bourgeois(ie) as Concept and Reality." In *Race, Nation, Class.* Ed. Etienne Balibar and Immanuel Wallerstein. London: Routledge, 1991. 135–52.

Ward, Mary A. "Introduction to the Haworth Edition of *The Professor.*" Rept. in *Critical Essays on Charlotte Brontë.* Ed. Barbara Timm Gates. Boston: G. K. Hall & Co., 1990. 101–3.

Welsh, Alexander. "Writing and Copying in the Age of Steam." *Victorian Literature and Society: Essays in Honor of Richard D. Altick.* Ed. James Kincaid and Albert J. Kuhn. Columbus: The Ohio State University Press, 1983. 30–45.

———. *From Copyright to Copperfield: The Identity of Dickens.* Cambridge, Mass.: Harvard University Press, 1987.

Westoby, Adam. "Mental Work, Education, and the Division of Labor." *Intellectuals, Universities, and the State in Western Modern Societies.* Ed. Ron Eyerman et al. Berkeley: University of California Press, 1987. 127–53.

Wicke, Jennifer. *Advertising Fictions: Literature, Advertisement, and Social Reading.* New York: Columbia University Press, 1988.

Wiener, Martin J. *English Culture and the Decline of the Industrial Spirit, 1850–1980.* Cambridge: Cambridge University Press, 1981.

Williams, Jeffrey J. "Smart." *the minnesota review* 61–62 (2004). 171–90.

———. "The Life of the Mind and the Academic Situation." In *The Institution of Literature.* Albany: SUNY Press, 2002. 203–25.

Williams, Raymond. *Culture and Society: 1780–1950.* New York: Columbia University Press, 1983.

Winnicott, D. W. *Playing and Reality.* London: Tavistock Publications, 1971.

Wise, Thomas James and John Alex Symington, eds. *The Brontë's: Their Lives, Friendships, and Correspondence.* Oxford: Shakespeare, 1932. 4 vols.

Woodmansee, Martha. *Art, the Author, and the Marketplace.* New York: Columbia University Press, 1994.

Wooldridge, Adrian. *Measuring the Mind; Education and Psychology in England, c. 1860.* Cambridge: Cambridge University Press, 1994.

Wright, Alex. "From Ivory Tower to Academic Sweatshop." *Salon* (Jan. 26, 2005). www.salon.com/tech/feature/2005/01/26/distance_learning/index_np.html

Index

VICTORIAN CRITICAL INTERVENTIONS
Donald E. Hall, Series Editor

This series showcases provocative contributions to Victorian cultural studies that make brash and revisionary claims. Pertinent manuscripts examine any of a wide variety of "texts": literary, religious, political/historical, art- or music-related, gender/sexuality-related, science- or class-related, or even that of Victorian studies itself.

Detecting the Nation: Fictions of Detection and the Imperial Venture
Caroline Reitz